THE SECOND INTEGRATION THAT TRANSFORMS CHINA
Theoretical Innovation and Practice in Building the Modern Civilization of the Chinese Nation

改变中国的"第二个结合"

建设中华民族现代文明的理论创新与实践

新华社"第二个结合"课题组 著

新华出版社

图书在版编目（CIP）数据

改变中国的"第二个结合"：建设中华民族现代文明的理论创新与实践 / 新华社"第二个结合"课题组著. -- 北京：新华出版社，2023.8（2025.2重印）
ISBN 978-7-5166-6983-9

Ⅰ.①改… Ⅱ.①新… Ⅲ.①马克思主义－发展－研究－中国②中华文化－研究
Ⅳ.①D61②K203

中国国家版本馆CIP数据核字（2023）第165829号

改变中国的"第二个结合"：建设中华民族现代文明的理论创新与实践
作　　者：新华社"第二个结合"课题组

出 版 人：匡乐成	选题统筹：许　新
责任编辑：张　谦　樊文睿	封面设计：今亮后声

出版发行：新华出版社
地　　址：北京石景山区京原路8号　　邮　　编：100040
网　　址：http://www.xinhuapub.com
经　　销：新华书店、新华出版社天猫旗舰店、京东旗舰店及各大网店
购书热线：010－63077122　　中国新闻书店购书热线：010－63072012

照　　排：六合方圆
印　　刷：大厂回族自治县众邦印务有限公司
成品尺寸：170mm×240mm
印　　张：16　　　　　　　　　　字　　数：160千字
版　　次：2023年11月第一版　　印　　次：2025年2月第二次印刷
书　　号：ISBN 978-7-5166-6983-9
定　　价：78.00元

版权专有，侵权必究。如有质量问题，请与出版社联系调换：010-63077124

导　言 / 001

第一章　"第二个结合"的丰富内涵与生动实践 / 006

　　一、尚"道"：信仰信念与千年理想有机结合 / 007

　　二、崇"礼"：制度成熟定型与礼乐文明有机结合 / 010

　　三、重"民"：发展思想与民本理念有机结合 / 013

　　四、敬"德"：核心价值与传统道德取向有机结合 / 015

　　五、修"文"：先进文化与优秀传统文化有机结合 / 018

　　六、贵"和"：命运与共与协和万邦有机结合 / 021

第二章　"第二个结合"的历史根脉与创新创造 / 026

　　一、找准契合点：日用不觉深入社会肌理 / 027

　　二、赓续根和魂：风云时变中把稳新航向 / 029

　　三、激活生命力："两通""两创"架设桥梁 / 032

　　四、助推新飞跃：理论创造与时俱进 / 036

　　五、创造新形态：为人类文明贡献新篇 / 039

改变中国的"第二个结合" —— 建设中华民族现代文明的理论创新与实践

第三章 实现"第二个结合"的科学路径与推进方略 / 044

  一、准确把握坚持马克思主义指导地位 / 044

  二、准确把握文化本质属性 / 045

  三、准确把握文化根本作用 / 046

  四、准确把握中华优秀传统文化定位 / 047

  五、准确把握文化传承发展内在规律 / 048

  六、准确把握中华优秀传统文化精华 / 049

  七、准确把握科学的世界观和方法论 / 050

  八、准确把握中华优秀传统文化同科学社会主义价值观高度契合 / 050

  九、准确把握中华优秀传统文化中治国理政智慧 / 051

  十、准确把握世界文明交流互鉴演进趋势 / 052

第四章 "第二个结合"的世界意义及时代启示 / 056

  一、何以中国：以文化文明维护世界和平稳定 / 057

  二、文治之道：把握六对关系应对治理挑战 / 059

  三、和合共生：文明新形态贡献人类美好新未来 / 064

结 语 / 070

编写说明与致谢 / 071

"第二个结合"智库报告发布研讨会专家发言摘要

傅　华：解读阐释宣传"第二个结合"，是新华社的重要文化使命 / 074

王均伟：从五方面深刻领会"第二个结合"的重大意义 / 077

李君如："第二个结合"破除了"西方中心主义"的思想禁锢 / 080

张志强：充分认识"第二个结合"的伟大意义 / 083

臧峰宇：从破解"古今中西之争"和实现"旧邦新命"角度谈对
　　　　"第二个结合"的理解 / 086

于运全：推动文明互鉴 增强中华文化传播力影响力 / 088

王学斌：三个方面着力继续推进"第二个结合"研究 / 091

马克·力文：马克思主义加中国历史文化特征等于中国特色社会主义 / 093

安娜·马林博格－乌伊：中国是发展中世界的光辉榜样 / 094

明竺：中国的经验对于发展中国家非常有借鉴意义 / 094

新华社大型纪录片《大道之源：改变中国的"第二个结合"》

第一集　文化根魂 / 099

第二集　治理智慧 / 112

第三集　文明之光 / 124

Contents

Introduction / 137

Chapter I The Rich Connotation and Vigorous Practice of the "Second Integration" / 143

1. Upholding the Way: Organic Integration of Beliefs and Millennia-old Ideals / 144
2. Advocating Etiquette: Organic Integration of Institutional Formation and Ritual-and-music Civilization / 149
3. Putting People First: Organic Integration of Development Philosophy and People-centered Doctrine / 154
4. Respecting Morality: Organic Integration of Core Values and Traditional Moral Orientation / 157
6. Valuing Harmony: Organic Integration of the Concept of a Human Community with a Shared Future and the Path of Harmonious Coexistence Among Nations / 166

Chapter II Historical Roots and Innovation of the "Second Integration" / 173

1. Identifying the Point of Convergence: Penetrating the Social Fabric Unconsciously / 174
2. Keeping the Root and Spirit Alive: Steadily Charting a New Course Amid Changing Times / 178
3. Restoring Vitality: Building Bridges through "Two Inclusions" and "Two Innovations" / 183
4. Facilitating New Leaps Forward: Exploring Innovative Theories in Step with the Times / 190

Chapter III Reliable Path to and Promotion Strategy for the "Second Integration" / 202

1. Upholding the Guiding Role of Marxism / 203
2. Essential Attributes of Culture / 204
3. Fundamental Role of Culture / 206
4. Positioning of Fine Traditional Chinese Culture / 207
5. Intrinsic Laws of Cultural Inheritance and Development / 208
6. Best of Fine Traditional Chinese Culture / 209
7. Scientific Worldview and Methodology / 211
8. High Compatibility between Fine Traditional Chinese Culture and Values of Scientific Socialism / 212
9. Wisdom of Governance in Fine Traditional Chinese Culture / 213
10. Trends of Exchanges and Mutual Learning between Civilizations / 215

Chapter IV Global Significance and Inspiration for the Times from the "Second Integration" / 218

1. China's Commitment to World Peace and Stability with Cultural Strength / 219
2. Chinese Way of Governance: Managing Challenges from the Six Dialectical Relationships / 223
3. Harmonious Coexistence: Contributing to a Better Future with a New Form of Human Advancement / 231

Conclusion / 239

Writing Explanation and Acknowledgements / 241

Project Team and Acknowledgments / 244

导 言

"这个古老文化忽然间充满了活力，充满了力量，这是个谜。"德国政治思想家施密特曾经在一次公开访谈中讲到中国时感叹，"没人能想到。"超大规模，又具有高度凝聚力，"两大奇迹"不可思议。安全、稳定、发展、进步。上万年文化，五千多年文明，绵延至今充满生机……

这个令全世界关注的中国之谜，如何解答？

"如果没有中华五千年文明，哪里有什么中国特色？如果不是中国特色，哪有我们今天这么成功的中国特色社会主义道路？" 2021年3月22日，中共中央总书记习近平在福建武夷山朱熹园考察时这样说。

"石破天惊！"给总书记做现场讲解员的文史专家张建光回顾当时心境，"我感到这将是载入中国共产党历史的一个重大时刻。"①

读懂今日中国，关键在于读懂中国共产党；读懂中国共产党，要读懂他所生长的文化文明土壤。

在中共理论发展史上，自上世纪40年代以来就有"把马克思主义基本原理同中国具体实际相结合"的总结，它成功指导了中国共产党领导人民革命、建设、改革的伟大实践，被今天的中共党史专家称为"第一个结合"。2021年7月1日，在庆祝中国共产党成立100周年大会上的讲话中，习近平正式提出，把马克思主义基本原理"同中华优秀传统文化相结合"，即"第二个结合"。

这个创新理论准确把握当今的国际国内大势，顺应中华民族伟大复兴的历史进程，展现了中共十八大以来，中国领导人勇立时代潮头，高瞻远瞩，朝着构建人类命运共同体的伟大愿景，带领中国人民重构史观、重塑认同、重释文明，逻辑自洽地阐释今日中国之治。

正如习近平2023年6月2日在北京出席文化传承发展座谈会并发表重要讲话时强调，"我们的社会主义为什么不一样？为什么能够生机勃勃充满活力？关键就在于中国特色，中国特色的关键就在于两个结合""结合不是拼盘，不是简单的物理反应，而是深刻的化学反应，造就了一个有机统一的新的文化生命体"。

本报告认为，"第二个结合"将共产主义信仰、社会主义信念与中华民族千年理想有机结合，中国特色社会主义制度成熟定型与礼乐文明有机结合，以人民为中心的发展思想与贯穿中华五千年的民本思想有机结合，社会主义核心价值观与中华民族传统价值取向有机结合，社会主义先进文化与中华优秀传统文化有机结合，人类命运共同体理念与协和万邦的邦交之道有机结合，实现了马克思主义与中华优秀传统文化"互相成就"。

"第二个结合"理论从中国历史深处走来，它找准了马克思主义和中华优秀传统文化的契合点，赓续了中华民族的根和魂，激活了传统文化的生命力，助推了马克思主义中国化新飞跃，必将有力推动建设中华民族现代文明，创造人类文明新形态。

什么是实现"第二个结合"的科学路径？本报告将其梳理为十个"准确把握"的方法论。

作为体量规模仍在可观增长的全球大国，中国的治国方略和观念变革，不仅在深刻改变中国，也将深远影响世界。"第二个结合"理论与实践使世界看到，中国的成长会一如既往为世界提供和平发展的最大公共产品，为全球带来稳定性和确定性。同时，"第二个结合"视野下的中国治理经验，可供他国观察与借鉴。

"第二个结合"，开创了中共理论创新的新格局，开辟了马克思主义中国化时代化新境界。它是打开理解新时代中国之门的一把钥匙，是观察中国式现代化、人类文明新形态的一双慧眼，是读懂中国与世界关系的一种方法。

它是21世纪引领未来的中国新的"文"治之道。

> "第二个结合"是又一次的思想解放,让我们能够在更广阔的文化空间中,充分运用中华优秀传统文化的宝贵资源,探索面向未来的理论和制度创新。
>
> ——习近平

第一章

"第二个结合"的丰富内涵与生动实践

掠燕湖畔,中央党校,伫立有《战友》马克思和恩格斯、《我们的老校长》毛泽东、《总设计师》邓小平等雕像。2017年3月,中国古代圣哲孔子与老子的雕像《问道》落户,与原有的雕塑一起,好似在这所中国共产党干部培训的最高学府里,论道交流,行"不言之教"。

山东曲阜,孔子故里,中央党校培训学员研学于此。他们在孔府孔庙中,聆听儒家经典,学习感悟古代圣贤的治世之道。在孔子出生地,好客的山东人连续多年举办尼山论坛,欢迎来自世界各地的儒学与中国文化研究者。

19世纪欧洲的思想家,两千多年前的中国哲人,今与古、中与外、西与东,跨越时空,思想的交流、文明的对话,不仅在建筑与雕像里凝固,更在今天中国式现代化蓬勃发展的广阔大地上鲜活地发生。中国式现代化赋予中华文明以现代力量，中华文明赋予中国式现代化以深厚底蕴。"第二个结合"理论的丰富内涵与实践探索，在行进中恢宏展开。

一、尚"道"：信仰信念与千年理想有机结合

"第二个结合"通过把共产主义信仰、社会主义信念与中华民族千年理想有机结合，赋予中国特色社会主义道路以民族的血脉、文明的底蕴。

"大道之行也，天下为公。"中国古代经典《礼记·礼运》里的这句话，是千百年来中国志士仁人追求的治国济世之道。小康、共富、大同，是无数先辈英杰"修齐治平"的共同理想。

作为先锋型政党，中国共产党汇聚了全国英才。从 50 多名初创者，到 9800 多万名党员，中共百年来的成长历程，得益于马克思主义基本原理同中华优秀传统文化相结合。志士的千年理想化为"为中国人民谋幸福、为中华民族谋复兴，为人类谋进步、为世界谋大同"的信仰信念、初心使命。

（一）"为人民谋幸福"接续奋斗

2023 年 3 月，陕西延安南沟村，一场春雨浸润，大片果园迎来花期。村民赵永东正在林间忙碌。他家 20 亩果园，去年净赚 10 多万元。黄土高原上的这个偏僻山村，近年来发展现代农

业、乡村旅游，带动村民告别贫困，村里人均收入10年间增长近4倍。赵永东说："我们的幸福生活，是党带领大家靠双手奋斗出来的。"

经过接续奋斗，到2021年，中国如期打赢了人类历史上规模最大的脱贫攻坚战，7.7亿农村贫困人口摆脱贫困，历史性地解决了绝对贫困问题，创造了世界减贫史上的伟大奇迹，14亿多中国人步入全面小康社会，人均预期寿命超过78岁，居民年人均可支配收入超3.5万元。人民群众获得感、幸福感、安全感与日俱增。

站在新的起点上，锚定"人民对美好生活的向往"，中国正健全基本公共服务体系，提高公共服务水平，增强均衡性和可及性，扎实推进共同富裕，开启为人民谋幸福的新篇章。

浙江德清推进产村融合，缩小城乡差距，2022年城乡居民收入比缩小至1.58:1，成为浙江高质量推进共同富裕示范区建设的先行地之一。

（二）"为民族谋复兴"信念坚决

国际史学家指出，古代中国曾经盛世辉煌，经济规模长期居世界首位，近代中国却在世界现代化进程中落伍，并在1840年后经历百年沉沦，国家蒙辱、人民蒙难、文明蒙尘。民族危亡之际，中国共产党扛起了"为民族谋复兴"的历史重任，争取民族独立、人民解放，实现国家富强、人民幸福，走过百年奋斗历程，引领中国发生翻天覆地的变化。

2022年，中国国内生产总值稳居世界第二；制造业规模居世界第一；建成世界最大的高速铁路网、高速公路网；科技自立自强加快推进，稳步进入创新型国家行列。

（三）"为世界谋大同"理想坚定

2000年前，悠悠驼铃响彻丝路古道，开启中西文明交流之旅。

今天，"钢铁驼队"呼啸西行，满载货物的中欧班列再次将东西方紧密相连，仅2022年就开行了1.6万列，运送货物160万标箱。

2013年，中国提出"一带一路"倡议，推动构建人类命运共同体。近年来，面对世界百年未有之大变局加速演进，习近平提出全球发展倡议、全球安全倡议、全球文明倡议，强调中国发挥建设作用，有力彰显世界和平的建设者、全球发展的贡献者、国际秩序的维护者、人类文明进步的促进者的责任担当。

过去十年间，中国对世界经济增长的平均贡献率超过30%，成为世界经济恢复发展的重要引擎和跨国投资的高地。国际货币基金组织总裁格奥尔基耶娃说，中国经济发展势头良好，将为其他国家提供重要机遇。从独立自主的和平外交，到建设新型国际关系，中国在世界舞台的一系列行动，为动荡不安的世界注入"稳定剂"。

二、崇"礼"：制度成熟定型与礼乐文明有机结合

"第二个结合"通过把中国特色社会主义制度成熟定型与礼乐文明有机结合，赋予国家治理体系和治理能力现代化以秩序的规范、伦理的力量。

"礼序乾坤""乐和天地"。陕西岐山周公庙，每年都举行祭祀，追怀周公圣德。三千年前形成的西周礼乐制度，是中国人自古而今形成的宇宙观、天下观、社会观、道德观的重要源流。礼乐文明的传统在今日中国，形成新的回响。以坚持党的领导为最本质特征的中国特色社会主义制度，不断完善提升现代化的国家治理体系和治理能力。

（一）制度形成有效规范

2023年春天，关于北京中轴线申遗的工作在忙碌进行。文保单位与有关企业积极合作，运用高科技开发呈现"数字中轴线"，使之能更好进行国际传播，为世界理解。中国首都的中轴线，具有独特的文化象征意义，几千年"大一统"的共同心理，"致中和"的哲学思维，严整均衡的礼序传统，在此有了现代化的表达。

哲学家楼宇烈认为，百年前民族贫弱之际，为除弊启民，中国思想家批判几千年的礼教只剩"吃人"，这好比泼脏水把孩子也泼掉了。实际上，中国传统礼教有其善处。礼教的本质，

是让人们明白所处的位置，按照规矩规范行事。比如对"天地国亲师"尊敬，就是礼教之善，今天我们当择善明用。

良好的政治秩序是"礼序"现代化的关键。从国家治理角度，中共十八大以来的"从严治党"具有重大深远意义。

坚持和加强党中央集中统一领导，构筑起"党中央坐镇中军帐、车马炮各展其长、一盘棋大局分明"的政治秩序，体现出秩序与活力、稳定与发展的平衡。这是对中华民族几千年讲规矩、重秩序"礼治"经验的激活。

2019年，中共十九届四中全会审议通过《中共中央关于坚持和完善中国特色社会主义制度 推进国家治理体系和治理能力现代化若干重大问题的决定》，总结中国特色社会主义制度和国家治理体系具有的13个方面显著优势，突出坚持和完善支撑中国特色社会主义制度的根本制度、基本制度、重要制度，构建系统完备、科学规范、运行有效的制度体系，把国家制度优势更好转化为国家治理效能。

"现在的政治协商、民主决策、政治监督、基层自治等制度体系，既能看到马克思主义的政治底色，又能看到中国传统文化的历史投影。"中央社会主义学院学者高国升说。

（二）法治建立严格约束

面向国旗、右手举拳、诵读誓词，"我宣誓：忠于中华人民共和国宪法……"这是2016年宪法宣誓制度实施后，频繁出现在全国各地的场景。从国家领导人到基层工作者，凡是国家工作人员就职时，都必须公开进行宪法宣誓，彰显中国依法治国的坚定决心。

甘棠飘香，清风正廉。公元前约 1000 年，周朝召公首创了巡视制度。2023 年春，在纪念这位古代政治家的陕西宝鸡召公祠中，30 多名新提拔领导干部的家属列队谈家风说家教，集中接受廉洁齐家教育。

中共十八大以来，中国共产党以前所未有的勇气和定力推进党风廉政建设和反腐败斗争，10 年间立案审查调查中管干部 553 人，处分厅局级干部 2.5 万多人、县处级干部 18.2 万多人，风清气正的党内政治生态不断形成和发展，探索出依靠党的自我革命跳出历史周期率的成功路径。

（三）伦理示范贤能教化

社会敬贤达，家庭尊孝道，个人重修身。中国传统文化中的优秀伦理与社会规范在今天有着特殊的意义。中共十八大以来，在中国城市基层与乡村，"新乡贤"制度正在成为唤醒中国乡村、推动基层治理的有效补充力量。

山西运城万荣县高村镇党委书记王国强说，全镇人口 3.2 万人，"新乡贤"就有 800 多名，"新乡贤"是村镇两委干部的"后备队伍"，乡村干部要做"新乡贤"文化的牵头人。

浙江湖州织里镇依靠"新乡贤"力量组建的"平安大姐"

团队,运用中华优秀传统文化中的"调解"思维,依靠亲情、友情、乡情"说和调停",组建8年来累计调解纠纷1660余起,调解成功率达98.3%。

三、重"民":发展思想与民本理念有机结合

"第二个结合"通过把以人民为中心的发展思想与贯穿中华五千年的民本思想有机结合,赋予执政理念以深厚的人民情怀。

"民惟邦本,本固邦宁"。民本思想是中国传统政治文化中的重要组成部分,反映了古代中国的执政理念。

中国共产党坚持马克思主义唯物史观,深化"人民群众是历史创造者"这一基本原理,结合中国实际,对中国传统民本思想有鉴别地加以对待,有扬弃地予以继承,创造性地借鉴了朴素民本理念的合理内核,提出坚持"以人民为中心"的发展思想,丰富发展了中国特色社会主义理论体系,从政治立场、价值导向等层面,实现了对民本思想的历史超越和时代升华。

(一)发展为了人民

中国共产党根基在人民、血脉在人民、力量在人民。从诞生之日起,中国共产党就将"人民"二字根植于心。人民性是中国共产党最鲜明的底色。

"让人民生活幸福是'国之大者'""人民对美好生活的向往,就是我们的奋斗目标""江山就是人民,人民就是江山。中国共产党领导人民打江山、守江山,守的是人民的心"……在不同场合,习近平这样说。

民之所忧,我必念之;民之所盼,我必行之。作为执政者,中国共产党干部在工作实践中秉持落实这样的理念。

20年前,浙江绍兴就从市、县、镇三级机关抽调"驻村指导员"下沉一线,访民情问民生、解民忧纾民困,被群众亲切地称作"身边的政府"。绍兴市委常委、组织部部长王琴英说,当地目前仍有7000多名这样的干部活跃在基层村社、企业一线。

(二)发展依靠人民

"水能载舟,亦能覆舟。"中国传统民本思想将"民"置于关乎国家存亡绝续的重要位置。中共汲取"重民"思想精华,强调尊重人民主体地位,依靠人民实现经济快速发展和社会长期稳定。

战贫困、抗疫情、促改革、治污染、化风险……中国人民都是"主力军"。

国家治理中,人民群众直接参与制度设计、法律制定和政策出台,实现了真正意义上的当家做主。2020年8月,在"十四五"规划编制征求意见中,网民留言献策超百万条,有关方面从中整理出意见建议上千条。

甘肃临洮县是全国首批基层立法联系点，当地已完成全国人大常委会法工委交办的70部法律草案意见征集。乡镇干部杨信的建议，被吸纳进中国乡村振兴促进法，他说："基层干部也能直接参与国家立法，民主就得这样能看得见摸得着。"

（三）发展成果由人民共享

美国库恩基金会主席罗伯特·劳伦斯·库恩30多年来一直关注着中国的发展。在他看来，"以人民为中心"的发展思想是中共政策的基石，脱贫攻坚和共同富裕是其有力佐证。

新时代10年，中国14亿多人的温饱问题得到有效解决，近1亿农村贫困人口实现脱贫，超过4亿人进入中等收入群体，居民人均可支配收入实现翻番，建成世界上规模最大的教育体系、社会保障体系、医疗卫生体系……幼有所育、学有所教、劳有所得、病有所医、老有所养、住有所居、弱有所扶的民生愿景逐步化为实景。

四、敬"德"：核心价值与传统道德取向有机结合

"第二个结合"通过把社会主义核心价值观与中华民族传统价值取向有机结合，赋予民族精神、时代精神以价值的源泉。

"自强不息""厚德载物"，源自中国古代经典《周易》里的乾坤大德垂范至今，与众多典籍里的思想，汇成两千多年

来中国人的敬"德"传统，融入 21 世纪的中国执政理念。中华优秀传统文化中始终蕴含着明德弘道的精神追求。

人无精神则不立，国无精神则不强。中国精神是凝心聚力的兴国之魂、强国之魂，既包含了中国传统美德的精华，也包含了社会主义核心价值体系的精髓，生生不息，薪火相传。弘扬以爱国主义为核心的民族精神和以改革创新为核心的时代精神，成为推进中国特色社会主义建设的强大精神动力。

（一）核心价值为统领

怎样在新时代铸牢中国精神？2012 年 11 月，中共十八大报告中正式提出了社会主义核心价值观。高度凝练的"24 个字"分为三个层面：富强、民主、文明、和谐是国家层面的价值要求，自由、平等、公正、法治是社会层面的价值要求，爱国、敬业、诚信、友善是公民层面的价值要求。

"这个概括，实际上回答了我们要建设什么样的国家、建设什么样的社会、培育什么样的公民的重大问题。"②2014 年 5 月，习近平在一次讲话中这样说。

从文明家庭、文明校园的创建，到遍布城乡的新时代文明实践中心，社会主义核心价值观广泛融入社会生活的方方面面，转化为人们的情感认同和道德习惯。

甘肃嘉峪关一处社区新时代文明实践所的宣传栏里，展示着地方政府的治理创新。他们借鉴古代经典《管子》"以家为家，以乡为乡,以国为国,以天下为天下"的治理思想,提出打造"政治引领、法治保障、德治润化、自治强基、智治提效"的"雄关善治·五治融合"社区治理品牌。

(二)干部政德为关键

弘扬社会主义核心价值观,使民族精神、时代精神落到实处,重在先锋榜样的示范。中国共产党干部是社会的中坚力量,抓好这些"关键少数"的德育至关重要。习近平反复强调,党员干部要"明大德、守公德、严私德"。

大德在爱党爱国,公德在维护社会良好风尚,私德重在个人修身。

山东济宁探索运用中华优秀传统文化提升干部政德修养,精心打造干部政德教育基地——济宁干部政德教育学院。基地结合曲阜孔庙孔府、邹城孟庙等资源开发现场体验式教学课程,让学员身临其境感受优秀传统文化的时代价值,增强文化自信。中共中央组织部已先后12次安排中央党校中青班1300多名学员来基地开展政德教育。很多学员培训结束后,还专门带着亲友和同事再回济宁,现场分享和传承传统文化感悟。

(三)德治法治相辅相成

法律是成文的道德,道德是内心的法律。中国坚持依法治国和以德治国相结合,既重视发挥法律的规范作用,又重视发挥道德的教化作用，实现法律和道德相辅相成、法治和德治相得益彰。

通过自治、法治、德治相结合，中国构建了城乡基层治理新格局。全国49.2万个村民委员会、11.6万个居民委员会，都由村民群众自己选举产生。2021年完成的新一轮基层自治组织换届，数亿人投票选举产生了近280万名村（居）委会成员。

五、修"文"：先进文化与优秀传统文化有机结合

"第二个结合"通过把社会主义先进文化与中华优秀传统文化有机结合，赋予民族复兴根和魂。

"观乎天文，以察时变；观乎人文，以化成天下"。《周易》中的这句话被认为是中华传统文化观的源头。马克思主义文化观认为，文化源于人们认识和改造自然的社会实践，又反作用于实践。这与"人文化成"的中国思想内在相通。

在今天的中国政治叙事里，文化被分为三个部分：中华优秀传统文化、革命文化和社会主义先进文化。这三种文化的形成方式不同，存在时间的先后不同，但三者关系不是割裂的，而是最终融汇成中国特色社会主义文化。

"发展中国特色社会主义文化，就是以马克思主义为指导，坚守中华文化立场，立足当代中国现实，结合当今时代条件，发展面向现代化、面向世界、面向未来的，民族的科学的大

众的社会主义文化,推动社会主义精神文明和物质文明协调发展。"③传统就是原创,民族复兴的根和魂蕴藏在中华优秀传统文化中。

(一)以文化人:让古典浸润人心

在中国西部四川眉山的三苏祠,来自全国各地的游客常年络绎不绝,人们专程来拜谒中国古代文人的典范——苏洵、苏轼、苏辙。一门三进士,留下诗词文字受到千年传诵,凝筑了中国古典文心。

2022年6月8日,习近平曾来这里考察。他说:"一滴水可以见太阳,一个三苏祠可以看出我们中华文化的博大精深。我们说要坚定文化自信,中国有'三苏',这就是一个重要例证。"④

文化为群体生活提供规范、方式与环境。在五千年中华文明中,文化承担着教化向善、陶冶情操、凝聚人心的重要作用。围绕"举旗帜、聚民心、育新人、兴文化、展形象"的使命任务,中国各地文化建设精彩纷呈。

(二)以文化物:让历史赋能生活

西安曲江,华灯初上,大唐盛景与现代景致在流光溢彩中交相辉映。在大唐不夜城、长安十二时辰等主题街区,身着唐装汉服的游客如痴如醉,在盛唐文化的沉浸式体验中流连忘返。

"在西安,站在城墙上,闭上眼睛,风吹来的都是历史和文化。"走进街头巷尾、茶坊酒肆，西安人眉目谈吐间透出一股自信。

运营长安十二时辰的陕文投集团，一直致力于"挖掘历史文化的当代价值，探索传统文化的现代表达"。董事长王勇说，在文旅融合中，中华优秀传统文化是宝贵资源，旅游为文化添翼，文化为旅游铸魂，实现了历史文化"吸睛"又"吸金"。

让收藏在博物馆里的文物、陈列在广阔大地上的遗产、书写在古籍里的文字都活起来，成为中国文化遗产利用新趋势。近年来，"考古热""博物馆热""非遗热"蔚然成风，创意文化产品火爆"出圈"。文化传承文明赓续，在人民群众喜闻乐见、雅俗共赏中，实现了对生活的滋养赋能。

（三）以文化世：让文化革新社会

文化引领社会风尚。近年来，中国各地大力实施中华优秀传统文化传承发展工程，完善公共文化服务体系，创建文明城市，振兴文化乡村，在全社会唱响主旋律、弘扬正能量，人民安居乐业，社会安定有序，风气焕然一新。

社会主义先进文化与中华优秀传统文化有机结合，提升了社会的文明程度，促进了社会的开放包容，驱动了社会的创新创造。

"车让人"让出社会和谐，垃圾分类实现"物尽其用"；"新市民"同等享受入学就医资源；市民生活事务"网上办"，农民种植养殖"智能化"……新习俗、新风貌拉开了当代中国城乡美好生活的新画卷。

六、贵"和"：命运与共与协和万邦有机结合

"第二个结合"通过把人类命运共同体理念与协和万邦的邦交之道有机结合，赋予人类文明新形态以思想的贯通。

"讲信修睦""亲仁善邻""以和为贵""协和万邦"。中国传统思想中，蕴含着丰富的对外交往智慧。十年前，习近平提出"人类命运共同体"理念，接续了中国几千年来的外交智慧传承。

当今世界，和平、发展、合作、共赢的历史潮流不可阻挡，但和平赤字、发展赤字、安全赤字、治理赤字加重，人类社会面临前所未有的挑战。中国始终坚持维护世界和平、促进共同发展的外交政策宗旨，致力于推动构建人类命运共同体。在人类文明形态中，呈现出中国思想之光。

（一）和而不同：尊重世界文明多样性

"和而不同"是两千多年前传承至今的中国处世之道。现藏于中国西北陕西西安碑林博物馆的大秦景教流行中国碑，记载了唐代时期传教士在华传教史实，体现了中国对外来文化的尊重。

中国东南福建泉州素有"七教荟萃"之盛。直到今天，多个宗教建筑在这里和谐集聚，融入百姓日常生活。

文明只有姹紫嫣红之别，但绝无高低优劣之分。2023年3月，习近平提出全球文明倡议，为不同文明更好地实现包容共存、交流互鉴贡献中国智慧。树立平等、互鉴、对话、包容的文明观，倡导以文明交流超越文明隔阂、文明互鉴超越文明冲突、文明共存超越文明优越——这是中国面向世界、面向未来的"文明宣言"。

（二）志同道合：弘扬全人类共同价值

中国提出的"和平、发展、公平、正义、民主、自由"全人类共同价值，凝聚了各国人民的价值共识，不仅源自马克思主义思想，也吸收了中华优秀传统文化因子。

在促进和平上，中国组建起8000人规模维和待命部队，向近30项联合国维和行动派出维和人员5万余人次，成立中国联合国和平与发展基金，是联合国维和行动第二大出资国和重要出兵国。多年来，中国在各种地区热点问题上积极开展劝和促谈。

在推动发展上，中国倡议设立亚洲基础设施投资银行，推动成立金砖国家新开发银行；促成国际货币基金组织份额改革，参与新兴领域治理规则制定；大力帮助发展中国家寻找致富之路，积极分享自身减贫经验，多次宣布无条件免除重债穷国和最不发达国家对华到期政府无息贷款债务。

在维护公平正义上，中国不走殖民掠夺的老路，不走国强必霸的歪路，坚决反对霸权主义和强权政治，主张国家无论大小、强弱、贫富一律平等，主张以团结精神和共赢思维，应对复杂交织的全球挑战，营造公道正义的国际环境。

（三）天下大同：构建人类命运共同体

2022年2月4日，立春，这是中国农历二十四节气中首个节气。在这一天，北京冬奥会精彩绝伦的开幕式令世界惊叹。片片雪花汇聚一起，组成象征和平的火炬。人类是一家，命运相共与。这在新冠疫情冲击全球的背景下，尤其引人深思。

中国推动构建人类命运共同体，不是以一种制度代替另一种制度，不是以一种文明代替另一种文明，而是在不同国家间形成共建美好世界的最大公约数。这一理念不仅汲取了中华传统中"天下观""和"文化的精髓，也是马克思主义"共同体思想"的创造性发展。

"一带一路"倡议是推动构建人类命运共同体的重要实践平台。据世界银行报告，共建"一带一路"倡议将使相关国家760万人摆脱极端贫困、3200万人摆脱中度贫困。

疾病是全人类的共同敌人。60年来，中国累计向非洲、亚洲、美洲、欧洲和大洋洲的76个国家和地区派遣医疗队员3万人次、诊治患者2.9亿人次。

气候变化是人类面临的共同挑战。中国与全球各国开展气候对话和务实合作，取得了显著成效，为《巴黎协定》的达成、签署、生效和实施作出了历史性的重要贡献。中国已与数十个发展中国家签署了应对气候变化南南合作谅解备忘录。

注释：

① 新华社记者对张建光的现场采访，2023年2月23日。
② 习近平：《青年要自觉践行社会主义核心价值观》，《论党的青年工作》，中央文献出版社2022年版，第72页。
③ 习近平：《决胜全面建成小康社会，夺取新时代中国特色社会主义伟大胜利》，《习近平谈治国理政》第三卷，外文出版社2020年版，第32页。
④ 《总书记考察三苏祠，讲到三个关键词》，新华社，2022年6月11日。

在五千多年中华文明深厚基础上开辟和发展中国特色社会主义，把马克思主义基本原理同中国具体实际、同中华优秀传统文化相结合是必由之路。这是我们在探索中国特色社会主义道路中得出的规律性的认识，是我们取得成功的最大法宝。

——习近平

第二章
"第二个结合"的历史根脉与创新创造

百年来,中国共产党之所以能够历经考验磨难无往而不胜,关键就在于不断推进马克思主义中国化,坚持理论创新、进行理论创造。

中共二十大报告中指出:"只有把马克思主义基本原理同中国具体实际相结合、同中华优秀传统文化相结合,坚持运用辩证唯物主义和历史唯物主义,才能正确回答时代和实践提出的重大问题,才能始终保持马克思主义的蓬勃生机和旺盛活力。"

"六经责我开生面"。习近平提出的"两个结合",特别是"第二个结合",不仅是对历史的深刻总结,对规律的深刻揭示,也是对理论创新发展的正确引领,彰显出高度的历史自觉和文化自信,实现了马克思主义中国化时代化的新飞跃,开辟了马克思主义中国化时代化的新境界。

一、找准契合点：日用不觉深入社会肌理

"结合"的前提是彼此契合。马克思主义和中华优秀传统文化来源不同，但彼此存在高度的契合性。相互契合才能有机结合。马克思主义传入中国后，科学社会主义的主张受到中国人民热烈欢迎，并最终扎根中国大地、开花结果，绝非偶然，而是同中国传承了几千年的优秀历史文化和广大人民日用而不觉的价值观念相融通。

（一）价值观主张的高度契合

马克思主义的理想社会是共产主义社会。中华优秀传统文化以"大道之行，天下为公"的理想作为最高政治追求，以"民惟邦本，本固邦宁"的民本思想作为基本政治理念，以"修身、齐家、治国、平天下"为实践逻辑，贯通"普天之下，四海一家"的"家国同构"政治伦理。两者都期盼建立一个没有压迫剥削、人人平等自由的美好社会。

2018年5月4日，习近平在纪念马克思诞辰200周年大会上的讲话中，强调了在九个方面学习马克思。这九个方面皆能在价值观层面体现马克思主义基本原理与中华优秀传统文化的契合点。例如，马克思主义关于人类社会发展规律的思想，

即人类社会最终走向共产主义的必然趋势，中国古人则孕育过"大同"理想；马克思主义关于人与自然的关系，与中国重要哲学思想"天人合一"堪称知音；马克思主义关于世界历史的思想，与中国传统的天下观不谋而合，马克思主义与中华优秀传统文化也因此成为"人类命运共同体"理念提出的两大源头。

中共二十大报告进一步明确了两者在价值观层面的契合，指出中国人民在长期生产生活中积累的宇宙观、天下观、社会观、道德观的一些体现，同科学社会主义价值观主张具有高度契合性，这都使得"日用而不觉"成为"第二个结合"的重要特色。

作为当代中国马克思主义、二十一世纪马克思主义，习近平新时代中国特色社会主义思想，与中华优秀传统文化在价值观层面深深契合，因此能深入到中国人的心灵，融入中华文化基因之中。

（二）实践观与实用理性的高度契合

哲学家汤一介曾表示，马克思主义与儒学都是注重实践的学说。坚持一切从实际出发，理论联系实际，实事求是，在实践中检验真理和发展真理，是马克思主义最重要的理论品质，而中华传统文化也具有优良的唯物主义传统，从先秦的管子、孟子到清代的王夫之、颜元、戴震、魏源等，都提出了许多富有见地的唯物主义观点。中华传统文化注重实用理性也是中国人接受马克思主义的重要文化心理结构。

中华传统文化没有排他性，相反具有极强的"海纳百川、有容乃大"的胸怀，善于吸收人类一切优秀文明成果。俄国十月革命的胜利，使中国近代先进知识分子更为直观地感受到马克思列宁主义改造旧世界的实践伟力，他们纷纷转向研究、宣传马克思列宁主义。最早接受马克思列宁主义的先进知识分子将马克思主义的实践品格与中华优秀传统文化中经世致用的历史智慧融会贯通，在近代中国最危急的时刻，用马克思主义真理的力量激活了中华民族历经几千年创造的伟大文明。

二、赓续根和魂：风云时变中把稳新航向

"源浚者流长，根深者叶茂。""第二个结合"把文化视作"根和魂"，因时应势，将文化的力量深深地熔铸在民族的生命力、创造力和凝聚力之中。"结合"筑牢了道路根基，让中国特色社会主义道路有了更加宏阔深远的历史纵深，拓展了中国特色社会主义道路的文化根基。中国式现代化赋予中华文明以现代力量，中华文明赋予中国式现代化以深厚底蕴。

（一）延续文化血脉的历史选择

中国共产党既是中国先进文化的积极引领者和践行者，也是中华优秀传统文化的忠实传承者和弘扬者。早在新民主主义革命时期，中共第一代领导人毛泽东就指出："学习我们的历

史遗产，用马克思主义的方法给以批判的总结，是我们学习的另一任务。"

中华优秀传统文化是我们国家和民族的精神血脉，既需要薪火相传、代代守护，又需要与时俱进、推陈出新。习近平精辟地指出："中华优秀传统文化是中华文明的智慧结晶和精华所在，是中华民族的根和魂，是我们在世界文化激荡中站稳脚跟的根基。"①

中共十八大以来，以习近平同志为核心的党中央坚持辩证唯物主义和历史唯物主义，秉持客观、科学、礼敬的态度，扬弃继承、转化创新，努力使中华民族最基本的文化基因与当代文化相适应、与现代社会相协调。坚持培元固本和守正创新相统一，深入研究新的时代条件下出现的新情况新问题，在继承中华优秀传统文化的同时做好创造性转化和创新性发展，使得民族文化血脉不断延续传承、焕发生机。

（二）推进伟大复兴的科学选择

今天的中国正以巍然之姿屹立于世界东方，比历史上任何时期都更接近、更有信心和能力实现中华民族伟大复兴的目标。中华优秀传统文化蕴含着中华民族生生不息的内在力量，书写着中华民族源远流长的文化记忆，是实现民族复兴的文明根基。

没有高度的文化自信，没有文化的繁荣兴盛，就没有中华民族伟大复兴。文化自信是更基础、更广泛、更深厚的自信。"独特的文化传统"是决定走中国特色社会主义道路的"第一原因"。习近平把中国特色社会主义追根溯源到"中华文明五千多年的传承发展",用文化贯通了中国的文明发展史。他强调,国家治理体系,是在我国历史传承、文化传统、经济社会发展的基础上长期发展、渐进改进、内生性演化的结果,充分说明道路自信、理论自信、制度自信,说到底是建立在五千多年文明基础上的文化自信。

在文化自信的基础上,中共二十大报告首次提出"文化自信自强",进一步彰显了在推进中华民族伟大复兴道路上,文化作为民族根和魂的重要性。

(三)多元思潮冲击下的必然选择

当前,世界范围内思想文化相互激荡,社会思想观念深刻变化。改革开放以来,一方面,中国虚心吸取世界文化文明优秀成分,另一方面,拜金主义、享乐主义、极端个人主义等错误思潮不时出现。中国思想界出现了历史虚无主义、文化虚无主义风险;有人把现代化等同于西方化,把代表西方价值的所谓"普世价值"奉为圭臬,严重影响人们思想和社会舆论环境。

面对各种外部思潮冲击与内生风险,习近平强调,要"增强做中国人的志气、骨气、底气"。他多次指出,要从中华优秀传统文化中理解中华民族的精神血脉:"中华优秀传统文化已经成为中华民族的基因,植根在中国人内心,潜移默化影响着中国人的思想方式和行为方式,今天,我们提倡社会主义核心价值观,必须从中汲取丰富营养,否则就不会有生命力和影响力。"②

新时代社会转型境遇下,优秀传统文化在抵御多元文化价值冲击、培育社会主义核心价值观等方面起着至关重要的作用,尤其需要大力传承弘扬。

三、激活生命力:"两通""两创"架设桥梁

批判性继承是马克思主义者的方法论。习近平以马克思主义世界观和方法论为指导,继承和发展了中国共产党对待传统文化的科学方法,坚持古为今用、以古鉴今,坚持有鉴别地对待、有扬弃地继承,不搞厚古薄今、以古非今,努力实现中华优秀传统文化的创造性转化、创新性发展,做到把马克思主义思想精髓同中华优秀传统文化精华贯通起来、同群众日用不觉的共同价值观念融通起来。

(一)正本清源:重视传统绝非复古

文化虚无主义全盘否定传统文化,文化复古主义则全盘肯定传统文化,用"悠久传统"反对现代化,用"千古道统"对抗马克思主义中国化,将中华民族伟大复兴简单理解为传统文化的复兴,一些不良思潮,甚至借由"传统文化"之名兴起。

文化具有鲜明的历史性特征，是人类实践活动的产物。传统文化在其形成和发展过程中，不可避免会受到当时人们的认识水平、时代条件、社会制度的局限性的制约和影响，因而也不可避免会存在陈旧过时或已成为糟粕性的东西。对于中华传统文化，不能一股脑儿、不加分析地全盘照搬，只有剔除了糟粕、保存了精华，才是中华优秀传统文化。

先进的文化思想一旦被群众掌握，就会转化为强大的物质力量；反之，落后的、错误的观念如果不破除，就会成为社会发展进步的桎梏。中国共产党自建立以来，始终重视对传统文化中的精华与糟粕的区分。习近平站在历史唯物主义的高度，肯定传统文化的特点和优点，但又辩证地指出其缺陷与不足，强调要引导党员特别是领导干部旗帜鲜明抵制和反对关系学、厚黑学、官场术、潜规则等庸俗腐朽的政治文化。引导全社会积极培育和践行社会主义核心价值观，树立良好道德风尚，防止封建腐朽道德文化沉渣泛起。

（二）正心明道：以马克思主义激活传统文化

知行观贯穿中国传统文化，重点体现为"内圣外王"，自宋明理学以后，中国传统文化日益变得僵化保守，以知行观而论，儒生更注重"内圣"即心性修养，却忽略了"外王"即外在的"事功"，结果陷入"无事袖手谈心性，临危一死报君王"的困境，面对变乱，束手无策。

毛泽东通过光辉著作《实践论》，以马克思主义实践观激活传统知行观，提出"理论与实践相结合"。习近平在毛泽东的基础上，进一步发展了知行观，强调知行合一，以知促行、实干为要，并尖锐批评"当面一套、背后一套，口头一套、行动一套"的知而不行、知行不一"两面人"现象。

"习近平面临的难题是，不能使中国成为文化的流浪儿、精神的乞讨者，因此必须唤醒中华文化中的传统文化基因，同时又必须赋予其现代化的灵魂。"外国学者如此评价。[③]

面对世界百年未有之大变局，如何立足世界之变、时代之变，深入挖掘中华优秀传统文化的时代价值？答案是："第二个结合"。

"马克思主义基本原理同中华优秀传统文化相结合"，一个"同"字，点明了"第二个结合"中马克思主义的主体地位，运用马克思主义立场、观点、方法，以客观、科学、礼敬的态度，激活中华优秀传统文化，使之更好地与当代中国实践相结合、与民族复兴时代主题相契合。

中国共产党人正确认识和深刻把握了马克思主义与中华优秀传统文化之间辩证统一、交织共振的关系，按照辩证唯物主义和历史唯物主义的要求，通过"第二个结合"对中华传统文化进行了科学鉴别和正确取舍，才能使中华民族最基本的文化基因得到真正激活，进而与当代文化相适应、与现代社会相协调。

(三）正理平治：创造性转化、创新性发展

马克思主义基本原理同中华优秀传统文化如何结合？创造性转化、创新性发展是关键所在。以"初心"一词为例，最早出自晋代《搜神记》，意指最初的心愿、信念。

习近平在中共十九大报告中强调："中国共产党人的初心和使命，就是为中国人民谋幸福，为中华民族谋复兴。"湮没已久的"初心"一词，通过马克思主义党性思想与传统修身文化相结合，被赋予崭新意义，由此得以激活，激励新时代中国共产党人接续奋斗，"初心"一词也家喻户晓，被选为2017年度国内热词。

不只在政治层面，十年来，文化"两创"已经深入中国人的生活。

古典舞蹈《唐宫夜宴》《只此青绿》一经亮相，迅速"破圈"；《中国诗词大会》《典籍里的中国》，引发读诗、学典热潮；良渚、三星堆等地的考古新发现，点燃群众对文物的热情。2023年4月18日，敦煌研究院与腾讯公司合作推出了"数字藏经洞"，现代高科技激活了千年的历史遗迹，中国故事、中华美学让世界都能即时共赏分享。

近年来，放眼华夏大地，从传统戏曲到文物保护，从非遗传承到文史典籍，从传统村落到年俗节庆，越来越多的人在传统文化的创造性转化和创新性发展中找到文化归属感。

通过"第二个结合"，中华优秀传统文化得到创造性转化、

创新性发展，其中的思想观念、人文精神、道德规范被充分挖掘出来，赋予跨越时空、具有当代价值的新内涵。艺术创造力和中华文化价值融合起来，中华美学精神和当代审美追求结合起来。中华优秀传统文化的生命力被时代精神激活，得到人民群众的喜爱，最终推动了马克思主义思想精髓同中华优秀传统文化精华贯通起来、同人民群众日用而不觉的共同价值观念融通起来。

四、助推新飞跃：理论创造与时俱进

不断谱写马克思主义中国化时代化新篇章，是当代中国共产党人的庄严责任。"第二个结合"不断夯实马克思主义中国化时代化的历史基础和群众基础，让马克思主义在中国牢牢扎根。同时，"第二个结合"是又一次的思想解放，让中国能够在更广阔的文化空间中，充分运用中华优秀传统文化的宝贵资源，探索面向未来的理论和制度创新。

（一）转化力：推动马克思主义大众化

自马克思主义传入中国，如何处理马克思主义与中国传统文化的关系，就是重大的理论问题与实践问题。中国共产党人做出了科学的回答：中国的马克思主义者首先是"中国的"，马克思主义理论不是教条，而是行动指南，必须随着实践的变化而发展。一部马克思主义发展史就是马克思、恩格斯以及他们的后继者不断根据时代、实践、认识发展而发展的历史，是不断吸收人类历史上一切优秀思想文化成果丰富自己的历史。一百年来，马克思主义深刻改变了中国，中国也极大丰富了马克思主义。

"第一个结合"，实现了马克思主义中国化的第一次飞跃；"第二个结合"，以习近平同志为主要代表的当代中国共产党人，以高度的历史自觉和坚定的文化自信，深化了对马克思主义中国化时代化的规律性认识，以中华文明为源头活水，从五千多年璀璨文明中承继人文精神、道德价值、历史智慧的精华养分，把马克思主义的思想精髓与中华优秀传统文化的精神特质融会贯通起来，为中国特色社会主义厚植历史底蕴和文化根基。

得益于"第二个结合"，马克思主义更好地开启了中国化时代化的新篇章，既立足中国实际，又呼应时代需求，在具有"中国智慧"的前进方向上阔步向前。

（二）向心力：持续推动由大众化到"日用而不觉"

中华优秀传统文化所蕴含的哲学观念、道德理想、价值理念、经验智慧等，丰富和发展了马克思主义。在价值观和思维方式等层面，推进马克思主义基本原理同中华优秀传统文化的结合，使"马克思主义'在中国'"变成"马克思主义'化中国'"。毛泽东曾指出的"'化'者，彻头彻尾彻里彻外之谓也"，逐步成为现实。

正因如此，马克思主义拥有更为深厚的历史文化根基、群众根基，真正成为人民大众所需要、所认同、所运用的立场、观点和方法，最终同中华优秀传统文化精华贯通起来、同人民群众日用而不觉的共同价值观念融通起来。

立足中国，面向现代化、面向世界、面向未来，中国正巩固马克思主义在意识形态领域的指导地位，并通过发展社会主义先进文化、加强社会主义精神文明建设等方式，推动中华优秀传统文化创造性转化、创新性发展，融入社会生活的方方面面，不断提高人民思想觉悟、道德水平、文明素养，也让中国化时代化的马克思主义更具凝聚力、向心力。

（三）交融力：着力建设新时代"中华民族新文化"

1940年1月，毛泽东在《新民主主义论》中，提出建设"中华民族的新文化"历史课题。当前，"第二个结合"的提出，极大拓展了马克思主义中国化时代化的新方向、新内涵、新空间。借由"第二个结合"，马克思主义找到了中国化时代化的新路径，并日渐交融为新时代"中华民族新文化"的一部分。

在"第二个结合"的推动下，马克思主义浸润于中华优秀传统文化的话语体系之中，中华优秀传统文化的生命力也因时代精神的融入而激活。走出"马、中、西"的对立，马克思主义已扎根中国百年，如今又通过"第二个结合"扎根于中国文化土壤。

理论自觉、文化自信,是一个民族进步的力量;价值先进、思想解放,是一个社会活力的来源。既从中华优秀传统文化中汲取治国理政的理念和思维,又以马克思主义引领中华优秀传统文化在当代的传承和发展,沿着"第二个结合"开辟的全新路径,中国实现了马克思主义中国化的新飞跃。

五、创造新形态:为人类文明贡献新篇

当代中国的伟大社会变革,不是简单延续我国历史文化的母版,不是简单套用马克思主义经典作家设想的模板,不是其他国家社会主义实践的再版,也不是国外现代化发展的翻版。"第二个结合"使马克思主义深深植根于中华优秀传统文化,成为中华文化的重要内容,跳出了以往所谓"马魂、中体、西用"等传统"体用"窠臼,"结合"的结果是互相成就,造就了一个有机统一的新的文化生命体,让马克思主义成为中国的,中华优秀传统文化成为现代的,让经由"结合"而形成的新文化成为中国式现代化的文化形态。

(一)从结合到再造

有理论家认为,"第二个结合"理论是"新瓶装新酒"的重大原创性贡献,因为其绝对不简单只是马克思主义与中国传统文化尤其是儒学的杂糅,而是激活与再造,是"化学反应",

是基于中国立场、摆脱西方话语体系之后的重大原创性贡献，是全新的中国思想、中国方法和中国气派，是崭新的世界观和方法论。

中国式现代化是"第二个结合"实现的场域。1840年鸦片战争以来，现代化成为无数仁人志士孜孜追求的目标。"怎样实现现代化，实现什么样的现代化"是时代考题。"第二个结合"为中国式现代化校准了航向，指明了方向。

"第二个结合"站在了人类发展的哲学高度来观察文化，依凭中华五千年文明的历史厚度来看待文化。一个国家的现代化只有植根本国、本民族历史文化沃土，才能枝繁叶茂、历久弥新。"第二个结合"把共产主义信仰、社会主义信念与中华民族千年理想相融通，让中国式现代化具有了价值引领、文化底气和历史支撑。

（二）从文化到文明

"第二个结合"不仅是文化结合现象，更是文明交融问题。文化的印记镶嵌在人类的一切物质生产、发明创造和理论构建活动中，便形成了人类文明。中国式现代化深深植根于中华优秀传统文化，体现科学社会主义的先进本质，借鉴吸收人类一切优秀文明成果，代表人类文明进步的发展方向，展现了不同于西方现代化模式的新图景，是一种全新的人类文明形态。

中国式现代化在继承人类从农业文明到工业文明等人类一

切优秀文明成果基础上，纳入中华传统文化中以仁为己任、己所不欲勿施于人的人文精神，纳入天人合一思想和对自然的尊重，纳入和平、发展、公平、正义、民主、自由全人类共同价值，从而完成人类文明由工业文明向现代文明转变的重大突破。

"克明俊德，以亲九族。九族既睦，平章百姓。百姓昭明，协和万邦"——中华优秀传统文化具备世界主义的显著特色。而马克思主义从诞生之日起，也同样具备"全球视野"与"人文关怀"。在对世界大势的把握中，习近平敏锐而深刻地捕捉到这一契合点，高瞻远瞩地提出了"人类命运共同体"理念。这一理念是着眼人类发展和世界前途提出的中国理念、中国方案，符合世界历史发展规律，符合全人类的普遍心声，受到了国际社会的广泛赞誉和热烈响应。

（三）从化用到超越

坚持把马克思主义基本原理同中国具体实际相结合、同中华优秀传统文化相结合，是一个长期的历史进程。马克思主义与中华文明的不断融合，正在开启再造中华文明乃至整个人类文明的大时代。"第二个结合"体现了中国领导人准确把握世界范围内思想文化相互激荡、中国社会思想观念深刻变化趋势下的科学决断和治理智慧。

未来中华文明的复兴，只能以中国共产党长期执政的当代中国为前提。没有中国共产党，所谓的"文化中国"早已"花果飘零"，成为"博物馆中的文明"了。中国道路具有自己鲜明的特色，这个特色是由几千年中国文明的历史传承所决定的，但中国道路又是普遍的，包含了马克思创立的科学社会主义的普遍原则。因此，习近平强调指出："我们坚持和发展中国特色社会主义，推动物质文明、政治文明、精神文明、社会文明、生态文明协调发展，创造了中国式现代化新道路，创造了人类文明新形态。"

马克思主义是西方先进文化的结晶，源于西方文明又超越西方文明，具有广阔的世界主义视野。马克思主义传入中国，既引发了中华文明深刻变革，也走过了一个逐步中国化的过程。中国特色社会主义使古老的中华文明焕发出了新的生机和活力，大大深化了中华文明的内涵，扩宽了中华文明的外延，把中华文明推向了新的高度。

注释：

① 《习近平主持中共中央政治局第三十九次集体学习并发表重要讲话》，新华社，2022年5月28日。
② 《习近平在北京大学师生座谈会上的讲话》，新华社，2014年5月4日。
③ ［美］熊玠：《传统文化是独特战略资源》，《学习时报》，http://theory.people.com.cn/GB/n1/2016/0617/c376186-28453910.html

实践没有止境,理论创新也没有止境。不断谱写马克思主义中国化时代化新篇章,是当代中国共产党人的庄严历史责任。

——习近平

第三章
实现"第二个结合"的科学路径与推进方略

当前,世界百年未有之大变局加速演进,中华民族伟大复兴历史进程不可逆转。新的发展环境和历史使命,要求中国共产党必须科学运用马克思主义基本原理,继承弘扬中华优秀传统文化,推动"第二个结合",来应对新情况、解决新问题、满足新需求、推动新发展、迈上新征程。

"第二个结合"开辟了马克思主义中国化时代化新境界,代表着中华文化和中国精神的时代精华。如何找到"第二个结合"的科学路径?本报告梳理了十个方面。

一、准确把握坚持马克思主义指导地位

中国共产党一经成立,就把马克思主义写在自己的旗帜上。

习近平指出："马克思主义是我们立党立国的根本指导思想，是我们党的灵魂和旗帜。"中共十九届四中全会明确提出"坚持马克思主义在意识形态领域指导地位的根本制度"，旗帜鲜明地把马克思主义在意识形态领域指导地位制度化，并将其上升为国家根本制度，列为社会主义先进文化制度建设的首要内容。

只有准确把握住坚持马克思主义在意识形态领域的指导地位，才能切实保证"第二个结合"沿着正确的方向推进。坚持马克思主义在意识形态领域指导地位，具有唯一性、根本性、制度性的地位，任何时候都不能动摇、不能模糊、不能混乱。历史上许多政党的垮台、政权的瓦解、民族的堕落，首先就是从指导思想的混乱、意识形态领导权的丧失开始的。这一指导地位决定了中国特色社会主义文化的性质和前进方向。中华优秀传统文化的创造性转化、创新性发展，必须坚持马克思主义的指导，否则就会迷失方向。

二、准确把握文化本质属性

文化是一个国家、一个民族的灵魂。文化的一个基本属性就是它的价值性，具备人所认同的价值。文化的竞争，本质是价值的竞争，是价值观的竞争。中国有坚定的道路自信、理论自信、制度自信，其本质是建立在五千多年文明传承基础上的文化自信。中华文明在长期演进过程中，形成了中国人看待世界、看待社会、看待人生的独特价值体系、文化内涵和精神品质，这是中国区别于其他国家和民族的根本特征，也铸就了中华民族博采众长的文化自信。

只有准确把握文化的本质属性，才能深刻理解"第二个结合"在中华民族伟大复兴中的重大意义。没有高度的文化自信，没有文化的繁荣兴盛，就没有中国社会主义现代化，就没有中华民族伟大复兴。坚定中国特色社会主义道路自信、理论自信、制度自信，说到底是要坚定文化自信，这也是14亿中国人民形成强大凝聚力的重要原因，为全面推进中华民族伟大复兴提供坚强思想保证和强大精神力量。"第二个结合"，是中国共产党对马克思主义中国化时代化历史经验的深刻总结，是对中华文明发展规律的深刻把握，表明党对中国道路、理论、制度的认识达到了新高度，表明党的历史自信、文化自信达到了新高度，表明党在传承中华优秀传统文化中推进文化创新的自觉性达到了新高度。

三、准确把握文化根本作用

文化是一种精神力量，能够反作用于物质，最终可以转化为强大的物质力量，文化的软实力最终也可以转化为经济的硬实力。文化兴国运兴，文化强民族强。文化的力量，已经深深熔铸在民族的生命力、创造力和凝聚力之中，中华文明的五千年积淀给中国人带来强大的自信心和自豪感，成为自强不息的精神力量之源。

只有准确把握了文化的根本作用，才能有效激发"第二个结合"在全面建设社会主义现代化国家新征程中产生的磅礴伟力。在全面建设社会主义现代化国家新征程中，统筹推进"五位一体"总体布局、协调推进"四个全面"战略布局，文化是重要内容；推动高质量发展，文化是重要支点；满足人民日益增长的美好生活需要，文化是重要因素；战胜前进道路上各种风险挑战，文化是重要力量源泉。马克思主义基本原理同中华优秀传统文化的结合，将进一步发挥文化的根本作用，凝聚起团结奋斗的磅礴伟力。

四、准确把握中华优秀传统文化定位

中华民族在几千年历史中创造和延续的中华优秀传统文化，是中华民族的根和魂，是涵养社会主义核心价值观的重要源泉，也是中华民族在世界文化激荡中站稳脚跟的坚实根基。

只有准确把握了中华优秀传统文化的定位，才能在"第二个结合"中增强历史自觉、坚定文化自信。"历史和现实都表明，一个抛弃了或者背叛了自己历史文化的民族，不仅不可能发展起来，而且很可能上演一幕幕历史悲剧。"中华五千多年文明延续着国家和民族的精神血脉，中国特色社会主义植根于中华文化沃土，忘记历史、丢掉文化、抛弃传统，就等于割断了中华民族的精神命脉。坚定文化自信，增强对中华文化的认同，就能以时代精神赓续优秀传统，更好构筑中国精神、中国价值、中国力量，使中国特色社会主义道路具有无比深厚的历史底蕴和无比强大的前进定力。

五、准确把握文化传承发展内在规律

文化传承发展有其内在规律。它必须适应时代发展的要求和人民群众的需要，只有创造性转化、创新性发展，才能绵绵不绝、生生不息。创造性转化，就是要按照时代特点和要求，对那些至今仍有借鉴价值的内涵和陈旧的表现形式加以改造，赋予其新的时代内涵和现代表达形式，激活其生命力；创新性发展，就是要按照时代的新进步新进展，对传统文化的内涵加以补充、拓展、完善，增强其影响力和感召力。

只有准确把握了文化传承发展的内在规律，才能找到推进"第二个结合"的科学方式方法。坚持创造性转化、创新性发展，使中华优秀传统文化得到激活，推动马克思主义思想精髓同中华优秀传统文化精华的贯通、同人民群众日用而不觉的共同价值观念的融通，才能使科学社会主义理论有更为鲜明的中国特色，马克思主义中国化时代化有更为坚实的历史基础和群众基础。

六、准确把握中华优秀传统文化精华

中华优秀传统文化源远流长、博大精深，是中华文明的智慧结晶，其中蕴含的天下为公、民为邦本、为政以德、革故鼎新、任人唯贤、天人合一、自强不息、厚德载物、讲信修睦、亲仁善邻等，是中国人民在长期生产生活中积累的宇宙观、天下观、社会观、道德观的重要体现，形成了讲仁爱、重民本、守诚信、崇正义、尚和合、求大同的精神特质和发展形态。

只有准确把握了中华优秀传统文化的精华，才能找到"第二个结合"精髓要义的源头活水。中华优秀传统文化不仅是中华民族的精神命脉，也是涵养社会主义核心价值观的重要源泉，其蕴含的思想观念、价值理念、人文精神、道德规范，不仅是中国人思想和精神的内核，对解决全人类问题也有重要价值。准确把握中华优秀传统文化的精华，了解其精髓要义，就能更好推进马克思主义基本原理同中华优秀传统文化相结合，进一步明确需要结合的对象、内涵，一方面挖掘出中华优秀传统文化的当代价值、全人类共同价值，另一方面使马克思主义呈现出更多中国特色、中国风格、中国气派，更牢固地在中国大地扎根。

七、准确把握科学的世界观和方法论

习近平新时代中国特色社会主义思想以全新的视野从理论和实践的结合上，深入回答了关系党和国家事业发展、党治国理政的一系列重大时代课题，既讲是什么、为什么，又讲怎么看、怎么办，既谋划部署任务，又指导解决问题，生动体现了马克思主义世界观和方法论的统一，能够不断提出真正解决问题指导实践的新理念新思路新办法。继续推进理论创新的科学方法，即必须坚持人民至上、必须坚持自信自立、必须坚持守正创新、必须坚持问题导向、必须坚持系统观念、必须坚持胸怀天下，是习近平新时代中国特色社会主义思想立场观点方法的重要体现。

只有准确把握习近平新时代中国特色社会主义思想的世界观和方法论，坚持好、运用好贯穿其中的立场观点方法，才能深刻理解"第二个结合"的理论品格和鲜明特质。"第二个结合"源自中华民族五千年文明积淀，体现马克思主义理论底色，具有鲜明的中国特色和时代特征。深刻领会其精髓要义，才能更好把握时代要求、正确认识问题、科学指导实践。

八、准确把握中华优秀传统文化同科学社会主义价值观高度契合

马克思主义基本原理蕴含的科学社会主义价值观主张，同

中国人民在长期生产生活中形成的价值取向具有高度契合性。社会主义核心价值观既提炼了马克思主义思想的精髓，也蕴含了中华优秀传统文化的精华。中华优秀传统文化遇到了马克思主义而焕然一新、充满力量，马克思主义遇到中华优秀传统文化而落地生根、开花结果。

只有准确把握中华优秀传统文化同科学社会主义价值观主张的高度契合性，才能搭建"第二个结合"融通贯通的桥梁和纽带。"第二个结合"是马克思主义中国化时代化进入新境界的重要方法和科学路径。只有找到马克思主义基本原理同中华优秀传统文化的内在关系，两者才能互相吸引，互相激活，互相促进，实现马克思主义理论、原理同中华优秀传统文化全方位、全覆盖的结合，最终融为一体，为丰富和发展马克思主义作出原创性贡献。

九、准确把握中华优秀传统文化中治国理政智慧

中华优秀传统文化是中国共产党治国理政的重要思想文化源泉。在几千年的历史演进中，中华民族形成了关于国家制度和国家治理的丰富思想，中华优秀传统文化中也包含着丰富的哲学社会科学内容、治国理政智慧，为古人认识世界、改造世界提供了重要依据，也为坚持和完善中国特色社会主义制度、推进国家治理体系和治理能力现代化提供了有益借鉴。

只有准确把握中华优秀传统文化中的治国理政智慧，才能明确"第二个结合"在国家治理体系和治理能力现代化中的历史方位。中国共产党在治国理政中，敬畏历史，敬畏文化，既不做历史虚无主义者，也不做文化虚无主义者，不数典忘祖，不妄自菲薄，善于从中华优秀传统文化中汲取治国理政、安邦济世的智慧。同时，用马克思主义的立场、观点、方法观察时代、把握时代、引领时代，不断深化对共产党执政规律、社会主义建设规律、人类社会发展规律的认识，这些是中国共产党执政兴国的重要经验，也是实现"第二个结合"的实践探索。

十、准确把握世界文明交流互鉴演进趋势

交流互鉴是文明发展的本质要求。当今世界不同国家、不同地区各具特色的现代化道路，植根于丰富多样、源远流长的文明传承。人类社会创造的各种文明，都闪烁着璀璨光芒，为各国现代化积蓄了厚重底蕴、赋予了鲜明特质，并跨越时空、超越国界，共同为人类社会进步作出了重要贡献。

只有准确把握世界文明交流互鉴的趋势，才能推动"第二个结合"在构建人类命运共同体、弘扬全人类共同价值中作出更大的世界性贡献。万物并育而不相害，道并行而不相悖。在推动人类文明发展进步上，中国不仅贡献文明新形态，还贡献文明新理念。和平、发展、公平、正义、民主、自由这些全人

类的共同价值，就是穿越时空、照临四方的中华优秀传统文化核心理念。中国还致力于推动文明交流互鉴，以文明交流超越文明隔阂，以文明互鉴超越文明冲突，以文明包容超越文明优越，倡导世界各国重视文明传承和创新、挖掘本国历史文化的时代价值，促进人类文明持续进步。

中华文明具有突出的和平性,从根本上决定了中国始终是世界和平的建设者、全球发展的贡献者、国际秩序的维护者,决定了中国不断追求文明交流互鉴而不搞文化霸权,决定了中国不会把自己的价值观念与政治体制强加于人,决定了中国坚持合作、不搞对抗,决不搞"党同伐异"的小圈子。

——习近平

第四章
"第二个结合"的世界意义及时代启示

从国际视野看,"第二个结合"是新时代的中国文治之道。它从治国理政视角回答了"何以中国"的世界之问。坚持"第二个结合",以马克思主义真理力量激活源远流长的中华文明,马克思主义也从中华优秀传统文化沃土中获得丰厚滋养,具有了鲜明的中国特色、中国风格、中国气派。它让世界看到,中国走出的现代化道路,创造的人类文明新形态,有着深厚的历史文化和文明传统。基于这样历史文化与文明基因上的现代中国,以负责任全球大国的定位屹立,为世界之变、时代之变、历史之变提供了稳定性和确定性,是坚定维护世界和平发展的进步力量。

立足新时代,面向新未来,中国文治之道为21世纪的文明共处，为各国共建更美好世界提供了新的启示。

一、何以中国：以文化文明维护世界和平稳定

"第二个结合"理论的提出，是中国在世界百年未有之大变局和中华民族伟大复兴这两个大局背景下的新一轮思想强国之举。在这一理论指引下，中国从文化自觉走向文化自信，进一步走到文化自强。这反映了中共十八大以来，中国领导人勇立时代潮头，高瞻远瞩，朝着构建人类命运共同体的伟大愿景，带领中国人民升级认知、改造思想、更新观念，逻辑自洽地阐释了中国之治，以文化文明的力量，为维护世界和平稳定发挥建设性作用。

（一）重构史观：超越旧有观念，掌握精神主动

长期以来，世界历史中关于中国的叙述被"静止论""循环论""落后论"等论调主导。中国的现代化进程日新月异，而国内外关于中国历史和中国文化的观念并没有跟上时代发展的脚步。

学者郑永年认为，一种文化若能成为"软力量"，必须能够解释自己，必须能够让"他者"了解和信服，最终使"他者"能自愿接受。[①]

"第二个结合"理论，超越了近代以来西方中心主义和中

国自身旧有观念，重构了中国人对于本国的历史认知，能有效解释今日中国的成功现实，从而使中国人进一步掌握历史主动和精神主动。这样的观念变革已经影响到其他发展中国家的有识者。

"过去，我们都是通过西方的棱镜理解中国，现在不同了。" 2023年3月25日，马来西亚总理安瓦尔在广州举行的亚洲青年领袖论坛开幕式上发表视频演讲时指出，"以我们如何理解我们的文化为例，我们总是认为西方优越，我们总是被告知，为了进步，我们必须成为他们中的一员。但我们意识到事实并非如此，我们开始审视我们自己的经历，我们自己的历史，我们祖先的贡献。"

（二）重塑认同：应对时代挑战，解决身份困惑

当今世界政治陷入了身份危机，国家内部出现部落主义，国际秩序出现了全球化断层线，美国政治学者弗朗西斯·福山近年来这样认为。[2]

更多学者认为，西方式现代化带来的原子化生活造成人们心灵的失落。各国民众都在寻找"归属感"，国家在寻求"承认"。而通向"承认"的斗争则聚焦于身份认同，这时候的敌人不再是王权或资本，而是"他者"或"想象的他者"。这导致国家的内部治理挑战加大，国家间交往更加复杂。

中国领导人通过"第二个结合"理论，重塑了本国的文化

认同、社会共识，从而强化了国家认同和政治认同。以党领政的文化自信，进一步强化了道路自信、理论自信、制度自信。

（三）重释文明：建构中国叙事，推动文明互鉴

时至今日，文明冲突论依然在世界广泛流行。西方中心主义和白人至上论随着时间推移不断变换外衣，但其内核没有本质改变。西方主导的"文明"世界与"非文明"势力之间的双向对抗影响着国际关系走势。

从在联合国教科文组织总部等国际场合深刻阐释新时代中国的文明观，到倡议举办亚洲文明对话大会……习近平一次次向世界阐述文明交流互鉴的意义。文明只有姹紫嫣红之别，但绝无高低优劣之分。面对"文明冲突论""种族优越论"等论调，中国明确倡导尊重彼此历史、国情和发展道路，强调以文明交流超越文明隔阂、文明互鉴超越文明冲突、文明共存超越文明优越。

2023年3月举行的中国共产党与世界政党高层对话会上，习近平郑重提出全球文明倡议，着眼推动文明交流互鉴，进一步丰富和拓展了构建人类命运共同体的实践路径。

二、文治之道：把握六对关系应对治理挑战

中共二十大报告提出了"六个必须坚持"：必须坚持人民

至上、必须坚持自信自立、必须坚持守正创新、必须坚持问题导向、必须坚持系统观念、必须坚持胸怀天下。这体现了习近平新时代中国特色社会主义思想的世界观和方法论，正是"第二个结合"理论的生动体现。这种"六位一体"的方法论，深刻揭示了新时代中国文治理论与实践的六大辩证关系，是中国传统思维方式的现代化发展，也是马克思主义辩证唯物主义哲学的现实写照。它对那些努力应对治理挑战的其他国家，提供了有益参照。

（一）人民与本体的关系

古希腊哲学家亚里士多德曾说，人是城邦（政治）的动物。人只有在共同生活中，才能成为充分意义上的人。人在本体论上是相互关系，没有人在关系之外。

在现代社会，作为处理公共生活的良政善治，关键在于处理好与"人民"的关系。世界上没有一个执政党不把"人民"挂在嘴边，但能够在治理中把人民利益置于最高并真正落到实处的，并非普遍。

学者王绍光指出，"人民"一词是中国共产党人的伟大发明。在新时代，人民理论进一步深化和升华。这种创新理论，使"人民"获得本体论意义。中国领导人强调的"以人民为中心"，既不同于中国古代与"官本"相对应的"民本"，亦非西方语境中强调个人权利的"人本"，更非宗教观念下的以"神"为本，或者金钱社会中的以"资"为本。从中国的治国理政视角,"人民"居于"至上"之位,成为具有本体论意义的合法性来源。

2019年3月,习近平在意大利进行国事访问时提出"我将无我,不负人民"。2021年2月20日,习近平在党史学习教育动员大会上指出:"江山就是人民,人民就是江山……"中共二十大报告强调,要站稳人民立场、把握人民愿望、尊重人民创造、集中人民智慧。

哈佛大学贝尔弗研究中心等多家海外机构的调查显示,连续多年,中国共产党在人民心中的执政满意度超过90%。遍观世界政党,这样的治理成绩是鲜有比肩的。

(二)自主与外鉴的关系

今日中国安定团结、朝气繁荣的状况,固然离不开学习外来、拥抱世界的态度,但归根到底是中国人不做附庸国,坚持独立自主闯出来的天地。

"中国的问题必须从中国国情出发,由中国人自己来解答。"中共二十大报告中这样说。今日中国的成功道路是党领导人民独立自主探索开辟出来的,马克思主义的中国篇章是中国共产党人依靠自身力量实践出来的。既不能刻舟求剑、封闭僵化,也不能照抄照搬、食洋不化。

"凡属由无生有,打开新局面,创辟新道路,在其发源处,则必有一番精神存在。"历史学家钱穆曾这样说。③

"第二个结合"理论找到了这种自信自立自强精神的文化之源。

(三)创新与守正的关系

"周虽旧邦,其命维新"。中国自古形成的"日新"精神,在新时代"第二个结合"中得到了新的理论拓展。

创新要以守正为前提。以马克思主义基本原理、把握好中国特色社会主义之"正",与时俱进之"新",就不会失去目标,偏离航向。

如何把"第二个结合"理论转化为实践的发展能量,习近平提出了把中华优秀传统文化创造性转化和创新性发展的"两创"方法。这种方法不仅应用在狭义的文化产业与文化事业领域,更是逐步嵌入了中国政治、经济、社会、文化等各个领域的治理实践中。

(四)问题与理论的关系

问题是理论的先导,理论是问题的升华。在实践中发现问题,总结理论,用理论指导实践,改造现实。

如何找准问题?在哪些领域找关键问题?中共二十大报告聚焦五大问题领域:实践遇到的新问题、改革发展稳定存在的深层次问题、人民群众急难愁盼问题、国际变局中的重大问题、党的建设面临的突出问题。这些问题领域的发掘体现了中国执政者把理论与实际问题密切结合以及对国情世情的深刻洞察。这是中国文治成功之道的重要途径。

（五）系统与局部的关系

中国传统思维具有整体性和关联性。中国人相信，万事万物是相互联系、相互依存的。只有用普遍联系的、全面系统的、发展变化的观点观察事物，才能把握事物发展规律。

这种整体性、全局性、系统性的思维方式能够超越局部的、分科的、具体的思维，不为一时一事困扰，看清当前与长远、整体与局部、小与大的关系。

习近平多次强调，要"胸怀'国之大者'"，要有"系统化思维"。

"中国人的思维擅长全局观，正如欣赏一幅山水画，是先从整体再到细节。"美国基辛格国际地缘政治咨询公司副主席兼首席执行官乔舒亚·库珀·雷默曾这样观察中国。

（六）中国与世界的关系

"修文德以来之"是中国与世界相处的传统。"胸怀天下"是中国共产党人的情怀。

不同于把世界作为征服对象的西方世界观，自古以来，中国人以天下去理解世界。无论是"以天下为天下"④，还是"以天下观天下"⑤，是以世界为尺度去理解作为整体政治存在的世界，就是"天下无外"原则。在中国人看来，任何具有外部性的存在都是需要化解的问题而不是征服的对象。⑥

在构建人类命运共同体的愿景下，中国共产党不仅要为中国人民谋幸福、为中华民族谋复兴，也为人类谋进步、为世界谋大同。要拓展世界眼光，深刻洞察人类发展进步潮流，积极回应各国人民普遍关切，为解决人类面临的共同问题作出贡献，以海纳百川的宽阔胸襟借鉴吸收人类一切优秀文明成果，推动建设更加美好的世界。

世界好，中国才会好。中国好，世界会更好。新时代的中国，以相互联系、相互依赖、合作共赢、和合共生的态度对待世界。

三、和合共生：文明新形态贡献人类美好新未来

在庆祝中国共产党成立100周年大会上，习近平指出："我们坚持和发展中国特色社会主义，推动物质文明、政治文明、精神文明、社会文明、生态文明协调发展，创造了中国式现代化新道路，创造了人类文明新形态。"人类文明新形态是中国共产党坚持"两个结合"，领导中国人民在实现民族复兴、推进中国式现代化的不懈奋斗中形成的文明结晶。从"道"到"器"，这种文明新形态在不同层面已经传导至世界，并产生巨大的积极效应。

(一)观念之道:关于世界理想社会的新创见

美国学者菲利普·克莱顿认为,世界面临一系列资本主义自身永远无法解决的危机。全球已形成三大共识:生态危机、不加干预的资本主义的后果,以及"现代性之死"。⑦

这位对中国问题有深入研究的学者认为,习近平新时代中国特色社会主义的思想与实践,对解决人类社会的共同挑战意义重大。

在一损俱损、一荣俱荣的全球化时代,在各种可预知与不可预知风险与挑战加剧的背景下,什么才是国际社会的理想状态?该怎样擘画人类的共同未来?

历史显示,引领者对世界的想象方式往往决定了现实的呈现。人类命运共同体理念下,"持久和平、普遍安全、共同繁荣、开放包容、清洁美丽",是中国对更美好世界的宏伟构想。

从2013年到2023年,中国领导人提出了一系列着眼全球、面向世界的新理念、新创想:人类命运共同体、新型国际关系、全人类共同价值、全球发展倡议、全球安全倡议、全球文明倡议……

从一开始的困惑、忽视、观望,甚至抹黑攻击,到严肃面对、认真研究、广泛参与,世界各国对中国十年来提出的一系列重大理念的回应日益增多。

2018年9月18日,习近平在会见爱沙尼亚总统卡柳莱德时说:"中国提倡构建人类命运共同体,就是主张国与国相互尊重，平等相待，和而不同，合作共赢。中国人说，尺有所短，寸有所长。国家不论大小，各有千秋，都是国际社会平等成员，应当摒弃弱肉强食、赢者通吃的丛林法则。"

"和而不同""尺有所短，寸有所长"都是中华优秀传统文化中的思想，同时也体现了马克思主义辩证唯物主义的核心要义。不同文明之间应该互相尊重、求同存异、和睦相处，以文明共存超越文明优越，以文明交流超越文明冲突。

习近平说："推动构建人类命运共同体，不是以一种制度代替另一种制度，不是以一种文明代替另一种文明，而是不同社会制度、不同意识形态、不同历史文化、不同发展水平的国家在国际事务中利益共生、权利共享、责任共担，形成共建美好世界的最大公约数。"⑧

英国作家、中国问题研究人员卡洛斯·马尔蒂内斯说，过去十年，中国经济实力和全球地位显著提升，中国的外交政策符合国际社会对和平、进步与可持续发展的要求，符合构建人类命运共同体的要求，这与以巩固霸权为核心的冷战政策形成鲜明对比。

（二）实践之器：知行合一的落实机制

将马克思主义基本原理与中华优秀传统文化相结合，内化于心、外化于行，最终要在实践中体现。

过去十年，在外交领域，中国领导人在不断提出新理念新构想的同时，把理念落到实处。几十次元首出访，几十次主场外交，主办各种全球大型活动。二十国集团峰会、金砖国家领导人会晤、中国国际进口博览会、中国-东盟博览会、联合国《生物多样性公约》缔约方大会、全球网络安全大会……在中国主办和引领的各种国际活动中，中国的文化自信随之提升，文明贡献随之远航。

已经推出并建设了十年的"一带一路"倡议，是人类文明的中国新形态在全球发展领域的一种"物化"，是中国贡献给世界和平发展的重大公共产品。

2018年8月，在推进"一带一路"建设5周年之际，习近平用中国传统绘画语言讲到，这一倡议要从"大写意"转向"工笔画"。2019年4月，在第二届"一带一路"国际合作高峰论坛上，习近平提出要推动"一带一路"沿着高质量发展方向不断前进。

根据中国一带一路网最新统计，截至2023年1月6日，中国已经同151个国家和32个国际组织签署200余份共建"一带一路"合作文件。中欧班列、亚洲基础设施投资银行、丝路基金，中国倡议下的各种双边多边合作机制方兴未艾……十年来，这一倡议从理念变为行动，从愿景化为现实。

意大利学者齐奥瓦尼·安多尼诺认为，"一带一路"塑造了中国的领导者身份，并且以非霸权的方式整合现有世界秩序。⑨日本前首相安倍晋三认为，"一带一路"对于维护世界和平稳定、促进人类文明多样性和持续发展具有深远的历史意义。⑩

中国创造的人类文明新形态以实现人民对美好生活的向往为价值旨归，内嵌了中华文明民胞物与、协和万邦、天下大同的文化基因，对于发展中国家现代化建设具有重大意义和启示。

在变乱交织的世界百年未有之大变局下，即便是老牌发达国家也面临着新的发展需求。比利时布鲁塞尔当代中国研究所所长格拉茨说，中国既是一个发展中国家，又是一个新兴大国，这两种角色最终会将中国融合成一个"负责任的大国"。实际上，有远见的政治家已经在积极行动。

一把千年古琴，一首千年古曲，奏响今日的和谐乐音。2023年4月7日下午，习近平在广州市同来访的法国总统马克龙一起欣赏了中国音乐家用唐代古琴演奏的名曲《流水》。习近平告诉马克龙，这首流传上千年的中国古琴曲背后讲述的是一个关于友谊的动人故事。

"高山流水遇知音"。在"第二个结合"理论指导下，当代中国马克思主义呈现出勃勃生机，中国式现代化建设正在持续波澜壮阔地展开，中国创造的人类文明新形态以友好的姿态面向全球。

"未来之中国，必将以更加开放的姿态拥抱世界、以更有活力的文明成就贡献世界。"⑪

注释：

① 郑永年：《中国的文明复兴》，东方出版社2018年版，第188页。
② [美]弗朗西斯·福山：《身份政治：对尊严与认同的渴求》，刘芳译，中译出版社2021年版。
③ 钱穆：《中国文化精神》，九州出版社2012年版，第97页。
④ 《管子·牧民》。
⑤ 《老子·道德经》。
⑥ 赵汀阳：《天下的当代性：世界秩序的实践与想象》，中信出版集团2016年版，第5页。
⑦ [美]菲利普·克莱顿、贾斯廷·海因泽克：《有机马克思主义：生态灾难与资本主义的替代选择》，孟献丽、于桂凤、张丽霞译，人民出版社2015年版，第14页。
⑧ 《习近平出席中华人民共和国恢复联合国合法席位50周年纪念会议并发表重要讲话》，新华社，2021年10月25日。
⑨ Giovanni B. Andornino, The Belt and Road Initiative in China's Emerging Grand Strategy of Connective Leadership, China & World Economy, Vol.25, No.5, 2017.
⑩ 《推动中日关系得到新的发展》，《人民日报》，2018年10月27日。
⑪ 《习近平在亚洲文明对话大会开幕式上的主旨演讲》，新华社，2019年5月15日。

结 语

"第二个结合"理论的提出，解答了今天的中国治道"何以从来""向何而去"的重大问题。它不仅是一套理论，更是一系列实践，不仅指向当下，更指向未来。只有用"第二个结合"理论，才能解释好中国自身的历史正当性、治理能力及其生命力。如果脱离五千多年生生不息的中华文明，就无法深刻认识中国将成为维护世界和平发展的重要力量。

在世界百年未有之大变局加速演进的时代背景下，围绕全面建设社会主义现代化国家、全面推进中华民族伟大复兴的奋斗目标，中国需要在"第二个结合"已经取得重要成果和宝贵经验的基础上，继续推进"第二个结合"。

马克思主义中国化时代化，始终行进在路上……

编写说明与致谢

《改变中国的"第二个结合"——建设中华民族现代文明的理论创新与实践》智库报告由新华通讯社社长、新华社国家高端智库学术委员会主任傅华任组长，总编辑吕岩松任副组长，原副社长赵承任执行副组长，课题组成员包括刘刚、储国强、肖春飞、崔峰、刘丽娜、傅琰、李劲峰、梁建强、林晖、刘翔霄、杨一苗、王博、勿日汗、冯源、闫睿、童芳、张云龙、徐壮、郭洪海、许雪毅、冯子雄、马昌豹、刘爱虹、何慧媛、梁劲。

课题自2023年2月立项以来，历时5个月学习、调研、撰写、修改、审校完成。

在报告写作和发布过程中，中央党史和文献研究院学术和编审委员会主任王均伟、原中央党校副校长李君如、中国社会科学院哲学所所长张志强、中国外文局当代中国与世界研究院院长于运全、中国人民大学哲学院院长臧峰宇、北京大学习近平新时代中国特色社会主义思想研究院常务副院长孙熙国、中央党校文史部中国史教研室主任王学斌、中国传媒大学文化发展研究院院长熊澄宇、中央社会主义学院中华文化教研部副主任翁贺凯、中央党史和文献研究院《党的文献》副主编高长武等专家学者给予了多方面的帮助和指导，在此一并表示诚挚谢意。

"第二个结合"智库报告发布研讨会专家发言摘要

读懂今日中国，关键在于读懂中国共产党；读懂中国共产党，要读懂他所生长的文化文明土壤。

在庆祝中国共产党成立102周年之际，7月2日，新华社国家高端智库向全球发布智库报告《改变中国的"第二个结合"——建设中华民族现代文明的理论创新与实践》，并举行研讨会，70余位国内外专家学者、智库代表、驻华使节、媒体记者等出席，对《改变中国的"第二个结合"——建设中华民族现代文明的理论创新与实践》智库报告给予高度评价和肯定。

部分观点摘编如下：

傅华（新华通讯社社长、新华社国家高端智库学术委员会主任）：解读阐释宣传"第二个结合"，是新华社的重要文化使命

把马克思主义基本原理同中华优秀传统文化相结合，即"第二个结合"，由习近平总书记正式提出并深刻阐述，是中国共产党的又一重大理论创新。在6月2日召开的文化传承发展座谈会上，习近平总书记进一步指出，"第二个结合"是对马克思主义中国化时代化历史经验的深刻总结，是对中华文明发展规律的深刻把握，是又一次的思想解放，表明中国共产党人对中国道路、理论、制度的认识达到了新高度，历史自信、文化自信达到了新高度，在传承中华优秀传统文化中推进文化创新的自觉性达到了新高度。

作为党中央喉舌、耳目、智库,新华社把解读、阐释、宣传"第二个结合"作为习近平新时代中国特色社会主义思想宣传的重要入口,集全社之力,从多个部门抽调骨干力量,组成新华社国家高端智库课题组。课题组坚持以"学"为先,成立第一时间即赴中央社会主义学院(中华文化学院)进行"住读式"学习,在深学深悟基础上带着思考与问题,赴国内十余个省区市广泛调研,与百余位专家学者和业内人士访谈,全面了解和研究"第二个结合"理论在中华大地的丰富呈现,深入思考和探究"第二个结合"理论在新时代新征程上的重大意义,最终形成了这份近3万字的智库报告。

报告从"第二个结合"的丰富内涵与生动实践、历史根脉与创新创造、科学路径与推进方略、世界意义及时代启示等四个维度,全面阐释马克思主义基本原理同中华优秀传统文化"为什么要结合、能不能结合、怎么结合"等重大课题,系统梳理神州大地建设中华民族现代文明的实践探索,生动展现中国人民融于血脉、形于言色的文化自信:用马克思主义真理力量激活中华优秀传统文化生命力,有册有典地赓续文脉,唤醒了亿万人民对文化文明的绵长记忆和创新创造活力,新时代神州大地呈现出"郁郁乎文哉"的盛大气象;用文化治国理政,中国特色社会主义和中华文明史一气贯通,强国建设、民族复兴汇聚了五千多年的力量和智慧,马克思主义中国化时代化具备了更加坚实的历史基础和群众根基。

改变中国的"第二个结合" —— 建设中华民族现代文明的理论创新与实践

"周虽旧邦,其命维新。"创造新的历史是对历史的最好传承,创造人类文明新形态是对文明的最高礼敬。新时代新征程上,我们要在当代中国马克思主义、二十一世纪马克思主义指引下,巩固文化主体性,成就新的文化辉煌。新华社作为党的新闻舆论工作重镇,将始终心怀"国之大者",忠实履行党中央喉舌、耳目、智库职责,持续深化"第二个结合"理论与实践的研究、阐释、传播,切实担负起"新时代新的文化使命"。

一是发挥国家高端智库优势,持续做好"第二个结合"的理论研究和解读阐释。"第二个结合"大大拓宽了中国共产党人的思路视野,让我们能够在更广阔的文化空间中,充分运用中华优秀传统文化的宝贵资源,探索面向未来的理论和制度创新。新华社将发挥媒体型国家高端智库优势,深化对"第二个结合"的研究阐释,在助力理论创新和发展上作出应有贡献。

二是加强主流舆论引领,深入宣传"第二个结合"的重大意义和生动实践。科学理论在伟大实践中更能彰显真理力量。"第二个结合"既是中国共产党的理论创新,也是中国人民的日常实践。新华社将深入宣传好习近平总书记推动中华优秀传统文化全方位融入治国理政的伟大实践,引导全党全社会切实把"两个确立"的政治共识转化为"两个维护"的行动自觉;全面呈现好中国人民在生产生活中推动中华优秀传统文化创造性转化、创新性发展的生动图景,引导全党全社会把"第二个结合"落实到文化创新的进程中,贯穿到中国式现代化建设中,进一步坚定历史自信、文化自信。

三是加大对外传播力度，充分展现"第二个结合"的时代价值和世界影响。新华社是具有全球影响力的世界性通讯社，在海外有182个分社，拥有多个世界媒体和智库高端交流平台，具有全球传播、全球到达、全球反馈的突出优势。我们将紧紧围绕"第二个结合"的理论精髓和重要标识，充分挖掘蕴含其中的时代价值和世界意义，打造融通中外的新概念、新范畴、新表述，进一步做好中国文化、中华文明对外传播，展现好中华民族现代文明背后的思想力量和精神财富，为世界文化与文明发展贡献中国理念、中国智慧、中国方案。

王均伟（中央党史和文献研究院学术和编审委员会主任）：从五方面深刻领会"第二个结合"的重大意义

新华社智库外宣报告《改变中国的"第二个结合"——建设中华民族现代文明的理论创新与实践》聚焦"第二个结合"这一党的理论创新重大成果，从丰富内涵与生动实践、历史根脉与创新创造、科学路径与推进方略、世界意义与时代启示等多个角度进行了分析和阐释，视野宽广、立意高远，结构严谨、内容翔实，语言生动、表述活泼，突出彰显了媒体型智库报告"专家读来不觉浅，公众读完不觉深"的独特风格。

学习习近平总书记关于"两个结合"特别是"第二个结合"的重要论述，结合这一智库报告，我有五点个人体会：

第一，相互融通和高度契合为"结合"提供了前提和可能。马克思主义和中华优秀传统文化孕育产生的时空背景不一样，因此，要把二者结合起来，首先要看二者有无融通和契合之处。习近平总书记不仅深刻揭示了二者"相互融通""彼此契合""高度契合"的内在关系，而且具体阐释了二者融通和契合的一系列思想文化元素。正是由于相互融通和高度契合，马克思主义与中华优秀传统文化相互结合才能成为可能。

第二，"结合"是互相成就、互动共进的过程。"结合"是双向的而不是单向的。通过"结合"，造就了一个有机统一的新的文化生命体，让马克思主义成为中国的，让中华优秀传统文化成为现代的，在中国化的马克思主义的指导和实现了现代化转化的中华优秀传统文化滋养下，中国特色社会主义文化得以孕育形成发展繁荣起来，成为现阶段中华民族的新文化，成为中国式现代化的文化形态，为强国建设、民族复兴提供了强大精神力量。

第三，"结合"筑牢和拓展了中国特色社会主义道路的根基。中国特色社会主义道路不是从天上掉下来的，而是在党领导人民进行伟大社会革命的实践中得来的，同时也是在对5000多年的中华文明传承发展中得来的。通过"结合"，中国特色社会主义道路得以开创并不断拓展，而且有着坚实的实践基础和深厚的文化根基，有着更加宏阔深远的历史纵深。中国特色社会主义道路为什么不一样？为什么能够越走越宽广？关键就在于"中国特色",而"中国特色"的关键就在于"两个结合",在于既立足中国现实的实际,又植根中华优秀传统文化的沃土。

第四,"结合"打开了进行道路、理论、制度、文化创新的广阔空间。在长期的奋斗中,通过"结合",我们掌握了思想和文化主动,并有力地作用于道路、理论和制度,不断激发创新创造的活力,取得了中国特色社会主义这一根本成就和中国式现代化这一重大成果,创造了人类文明新形态。新征程上,我们必须以"又一次的思想解放"的高度和自觉,推动"两个结合"特别是"第二个结合"发生更多的"化学反应",勇于进行实践基础上的创新创造,特别是探索面向未来的理论和制度创新,为进一步丰富和发展人类文明新形态提供指引和支撑。

第五,"结合"巩固了中国共产党和中国人民的文化主体性。从"契合"到"结合"不是自然而然发生的,需要文化主体的自觉和主动努力。把"一个结合"丰富发展为"两个结合",有力彰显和巩固了中国共产党和中国人民的文化主体性,集中反映和体现了新时代中国共产党的自信自觉、自立自强,深刻表明我们党对中国道路、理论、制度的认识达到了新高度,表明我们党的历史自信、文化自信达到了新高度,表明我们党在传承中华优秀传统文化中推进文化创新的自觉性达到了新高度,从而为我们党带领人民担负起新的文化使命、建设中华民族的现代文明奠定了关键基础。

李君如（原中央党校副校长）："第二个结合"破除了"西方中心主义"的思想禁锢

新华社国家高端智库的研究报告《改变中国的"第二个结合"》，视野开阔，思考深入，语言生动，系统阐述了"第二个结合"的理论创新意义，具有很高的研究水平和学术价值。

习近平总书记今年6月2日在文化传承发展座谈会上深刻地指出："'第二个结合'是又一次的思想解放，让我们能够在更广阔的文化空间中，充分运用中华优秀传统文化的宝贵资源，探索面向未来的理论和制度创新。"新华社国家高端智库这个研究报告，对于我们深入认识"'第二个结合'是又一次的思想解放"，具有很大的启迪意义。

那么，为什么说"'第二个结合'是又一次的思想解放"呢？

首先，"第二个结合"破除了"西方中心主义"的思想禁锢。在"两个结合"中，我们知道，"第一个结合"是一次伟大的思想解放，主要是破除了我们党内长期存在的主观主义特别是对马克思主义的教条主义倾向。习近平总书记提出的"第二个结合"，和"第一个结合"联结在一起，不仅针对的是不从实际出发的形式主义、官僚主义作风，而且破除了"西方中心主义"的思想禁锢。在今年2月7日举办的学习贯彻党的二十大精神研讨班开班式上，习近平总书记明确指出："中国式现代化，打破了'现代化＝西方化'的迷思"。他强调："中国式现代化，深深植根于中华优秀传统文化，体现科学社会主义的先进本质，借鉴吸收一切人类优秀文明成果，代表人类文明进步的发展方向，展现了不同于西方现代化模式的新图景，是全新的人类文明形态。"

其次，"第二个结合"破除了"历史虚无主义"和"文化虚无主义"的迷雾。十月革命一声炮响，给我们送来了马克思列宁主义后，中国人在精神上由被动转入主动，那种看不起中国人、看不起中国文化的时代完结了，开始了复兴伟大的中国人民文化的新时代。但是，有人以我们的社会主义实践中出现的失误为由头，以历史虚无主义和文化虚无主义的态度抹黑中国革命的历史，以轻蔑的口吻否定中华文明的价值。自中国特色社会主义进入新时代以来，以习近平同志为核心的党中央一而再、再而三地提醒我们，要警惕这些错误思潮，强调要坚定我们的道路自信、理论自信、制度自信和文化自信。这次在文化传承发展座谈会上，习近平总书记进一步分析了中华文明具有突出的连续性、突出的创新性、突出的统一性、突出的包容性、突出的和平性，深刻指出："在五千多年中华文明深厚基础上开辟和发展中国特色社会主义，把马克思主义基本原理同中国具体实际相结合、同中华优秀传统文化相结合是必由之路。"他明确指出："'第二个结合'，是我们党对马克思主义中国化时代化历史经验的深刻总结，是对中华文明发展规律的深刻把握，表明我们党对中国道路、理论、制度的认识达到了新高度，表明我们党的历史自信、文化自信达到了新的高度，表明我们党在传承中华优秀传统文化中推进文化创新的自觉性达到了新高度。"

再次,"第二个结合"破除了简单延续我国历史文化的肤浅认识。习近平总书记在哲学社会科学工作座谈会和纪念马克思诞辰200周年大会等场合,反复强调"当代中国的伟大社会变革,不是简单延续我国历史文化的母版,不是简单套用马克思主义经典作家设想的模板,不是其他国家社会主义实践的再版,也不是国外现代化发展的翻版。"这段话在十九届六中全会通过的历史决议论述"两个结合"重要思想的时候再一次被引用。在这段话中,他不仅提出要正确认识马克思主义经典作家设想、其他国家社会主义实践和国外现代化发展的做法,而且提出要正确认识我国的历史文化。在今天强调要弘扬中华文明的时候,尤其要注意这一点。为此,习近平总书记一而再、再而三提出一个极其重要的命题:中华优秀传统文化的"创造性转化"和"创新性发展"。这次,在文化传承发展座谈会上,他进一步强调:"中国文化源远流长,中华文明博大精深。只有全面深入的了解中华文明的历史,才能更有效地推动中华优秀传统文化创造性转化、创新性发展,更有力地推进中国特色社会主义文化建设,建设中华民族现代文明。"提出"第二个结合",一个重大的意义,就是使我们进一步认识新时代的文化使命,在新的起点上继续推动文化繁荣、建设文化强国、建设中华民族现代文明。正如习近平总书记要求我们的那样:"要坚定文化自信、担当使命、奋发有为，共同努力创造属于我们这个时代的新文化，建设中华民族现代文明。"

与此同时，我们还要清醒地认识到，懂得了"'第二个结合'是又一次的思想解放"，为我们推进"又一次的思想解放"指明了方向，并不是说这一次思想解放已经完成了。我们面前还有许许多多问题要深入思考和研究。如何进一步从哲学上讲清楚"第二个结合"，讲清楚来源不同的思想文化是怎么在彼此契合中相结合的，还需要我们做更加深入的研究。

张志强（中国社会科学院哲学所所长）：充分认识"第二个结合"的伟大意义

仔细阅读了整个报告，感觉真是非常振奋人心的一个报告，关于中华文化思想的内容进行了非常系统地概括，对第二个结合实现了文化创造进行了非常精准地刻画。报告中更突出的贡献是，这个报告把"第二个结合"独立提出来、强调出来加以总结，意义十分重要，有助于廓清理论界一些模糊的认识。

为什么"第二个结合"具有如此重要的意义，是因为"第二个结合"它体现了新时代的一个自信自强的时代精神。

报告里边提到了三个文化主体性，一个是中华文明的文化主体性，一个是中国民族的文化主体性，还有一个是中国特色社会主义的文化主体性，还有一个总括起来讲，我们可以理解的叫中国共产党的文化主体性的问题。对文化主体性特别强调，应该是"第二个结合"里边的一个核心的主题。报告当中特别提到,"第二个结合"充实了马克思主义的文化生命,实现了中华文明的现代形态。用中华文化充实马克思主义文化的生命,让马克思主义成为中国的,就是在让马克思主义具有中国形式和中国的形态之外,进一步让马克思主义自身也具有了中国文化生命。习近平新时代中国特色社会主义思想作为中华文化和中国精神的时代化,就是具有中国文化生命的当代中国马克思主义。

智库报告当中第一次非常清楚地提出了一个概念,叫"中华文明发展规律",这是一个崭新的提法。习近平总书记在文化传承发展座谈会上指出,中华优秀传统文化有很多重要元素,共同塑造出中华文明的突出特性。中华文明具有突出的连续性、突出的创新性、突出的统一性、突出的包容性、突出的和平性。我们理解中华文明突出的特性,这五个特性其实就构成了中华文明的发展规律,为什么这么讲呢?这五个特性之间它不是偶然的,这五个特性之间是有一个系统性的、原理性的关系的。我们可以看到这五个特性在讲话当中讲述的顺序也是有讲究的,第一个是连续,第二个是创新。实际上,我们知道连续性和创新性之间就构成了一种原理性的关系。中华文明突出的连续性的特点其实是来自于中华文明一个核心的原理叫通史的原理,我们知道通史原理的核心其实在讲一个变中之不变,不变中的变,所谓的连续它一定是变中之不变和不变中的变，如果只强调不变就不会有连续，如果只强调变化也不会有连续，所以变化是变中之不变和不变中之变的一个关系，所以在这个连续当中它一定包含着创新的含义，这就是通史的意思，我们讲"随时损益、百世可知"的道理，讲通史的"通"其实是一个动词的意思，让历史不断通达下去，因此通史这个原理背后包含着历史主动性精神，而历史主动性精神就是创新性，也是中国传统里边的叫革故鼎新、晖光日新的革命精神的一个体现。

统一性来自中国文明里边的大一统原理，而这个大一统原理就是多元一体的原理，必然包含着包容性，包容性和和平性之间更是大一统原理背后所呈现出来的天下为公、天下一家原理的表现，包容必然是和平的，越包容越能够得到认同，越能够长期存在，这是总书记在讲话里面特别提到的包容性和统一性之间的这样一个原理性关系。而中国对于统一的追求是中国文明一个最根本的特征，统一是中华文明一个基本的特征，我们理解的第二个结合，马克思主义基本原理要结合的内容，其实就是要结合这五个特性，就是要结合中华文明的发展规律。也就是说，我们在结合当中所创造的中华民族的现代文明这个新文化一定是对这五个特性的维持、发展，是对这五个特性的创造性转化和创新性发展，是对这五个特性的一气贯通、与时俱进。也就是说不能够丢掉这五个特性，建设中华文明现代形态、中华民族现代文明，对这五个特性中任何一个都不能丢弃的，丢弃了就不是中华文明，这是我们理解"第二个结合"中"结合"的对象和"结合"的内容。

"第二个结合"昭示了一条建设中华民族现代文明的一个根本的途径。"第二个结合"蕴含着一层含义，是指马克思主义所揭示的社会主义建设规律和中国共产党的这个执政规律与中华文明发展规律具有深层次的高度的契合性。中华文明发展规律与社会主义建设规律的这种高度契合性是在坚持中华文明发展规律前提下，在深刻把握中国共产党执政规律是前提下，运用社会主义建设规律，创发出的更为普遍、更为根本的人类社会发展规律。"第二个结合"作为建设中华民族现代文明根本途径，也是在强调中华文明的发展规律与前三个规律之间其实是有着一种系统性的原理性的关联，而这一关联是从"第二个结合"所昭示的建设中华民族现代文明根本途径的意义上展现出来的。

臧峰宇（中国人民大学哲学院院长）从破解"古今中西之争"和实现"旧邦新命"角度谈对"第二个结合"的理解

《改变中国的"第二个结合"——建设中华民族现代文明的理论创新与实践》智库报告力图解答古老的中华文化何以在新时代充满活力这个重要问题。

——将"古今中西之争"转换为文化古今相通与文明交流互鉴

文明交流互鉴使我们更好地理解民族文化自我，在对话与会通中拓展了文化传承发展空间。这一空间的实践场域是传承发展中华优秀传统文化的中国式现代化，体现为中华民族作为世界历史民族承担的特定历史使命，确证了"第二个结合"的现实必要性，将古今中西之争转换为文化古今相通与文明交流互鉴，其所创造的人类文明新形态具有世界历史意义。

——实现中华民族"旧邦新命" 建设中华民族现代文明

中华优秀传统文化创造性转化、创新性发展取决于时代条件和实践需要。同马克思主义基本原理相结合的中华优秀传统文化，只有转化为中国特色社会主义文明，才能产生现实的物质力量。正是一经诞生就把为中国人民谋幸福、为中华民族谋复兴确立为初心使命的中国共产党，带领人民在百余年实践中改变了中华民族的前途和命运，实现了物质文明、政治文明、精神文明、生态文明和社会文明持续发展，使中华优秀传统文化浴火重生。

在新的历史起点上，我们要以新的文化使命与守正创新的正气和锐气，实现中华民族的旧邦新命，努力建设中华民族现代文明，使历史和现实交汇，加强东方和西方对话，在观念创新中形成构建人类命运共同体的文化合力，真正解决当今时代人类共同的文化问题，在塑造人类未来命运的期冀中铸就共同体的文化根基。

于运全（中国外文局当代中国与世界研究院院长）：推动文明互鉴 增强中华文化传播力影响力

——守正创新，开辟中华优秀传统文化传承创新新路径

坚持"两个结合"，创造人类文明新形态。科学和正确对待中华优秀传统文化，以马克思主义为方法论指导，在进行鉴别与分析、取舍与扬弃的基础上，实现中华优秀传统文化的现代化转化。坚持马克思主义基本观点和中国立场，加强对中华优秀传统文化的挖掘和阐发，使中华民族最基本的文化基因与当代文化相适应、与现代社会相协调。重视挖掘中华五千年文明中的精华，弘扬优秀传统文化，把其中的精华同马克思主义立场观点方法结合起来，坚定不移走中国特色社会主义道路。

坚定文化自信，传承弘扬中华民族数千年积累下的伟大智慧。增强文化自觉，坚定文化自信，最重要的就是用历史唯物主义的立场观点方法看待中华民族历史，继承和弘扬中华优秀传统文化。中国优秀传统文化的丰富哲学思想、人文精神、教化思想、道德理念等，可以为人们认识和改造世界提供有益启迪，可以为治国理政提供有益启示，也可以为道德建设提供有益启发。

坚持守正创新，以现代化视野弘扬中华优秀传统。以辩证的态度对待中华传统文化，坚持古为今用、以古鉴今，坚持有鉴别的对待、有扬弃的继承，努力实现中华传统文化的创造性

转化、创新性发展。坚持守正创新、推陈出新，注重运用现代科技手段丰富中华优秀传统文化的表现形式，让收藏在博物馆里的文物、陈列在广阔大地上的遗产、书写在古籍里的文字都活起来。

推动文明互鉴，广泛吸收借鉴人类文明成果。坚持弘扬平等、互鉴、对话、包容的文明观，以宽广胸怀理解不同文明对价值内涵的认识，尊重不同国家人民对自身发展道路的探索，以文明交流超越文明隔阂，以文明互鉴超越文明冲突，以文明共存超越文明优越，弘扬中华文明蕴含的全人类共同价值，推动构建人类命运共同体。

——多措并举，增强中华优秀传统文化传播力影响力

把握"两个结合"，深化习近平新时代中国特色社会主义思想对外传播。深入阐释中国式现代化、人类命运共同体等重大理念的文化根源，加强全球文明倡议的国际传播。全力推进习近平总书记重要著作的翻译出版发行，与国内外机构打造联合传播平台，全面展现中国文化和中国精神的时代精华。

协调各方力量，完善中外文明交流互鉴工作格局。在深入调研的基础上，对目标、内容、路径、渠道、重大任务和重大工程、组织领导、实施主体、政策支持、资金保障、资源统筹等进行系统规划，构建与中国综合国力和国际地位相匹配的文化软实力。加强协同协作，协调政府、专业机构、企业等多元文化力量，用好国际组织、民间组织、中资企业、华侨华人、媒体、文艺

院团和文博机构等资源,建设多层次文化交流体系。

开展系统研究,加强文明交流话语创新和叙事体系建设。深入挖掘和提炼中华文明中蕴含的思想、理念、精神、价值观等深层次内涵,展现中华文化精髓。注重中华文明中具有当代价值的思想精神和价值理念的传播,从文化上讲清楚今天的中国是什么样的国家、中国人是什么样的人。注重中华文明中具有世界意义的思想精神和价值理念的传播,从文化上讲清楚中国发展对世界意味着什么。

强化知识传播,实施中华文明对外出版工程。发挥对外出版在文化传播中的独特优势,结合国外读者关切,策划出版更多体现中国精神、中国价值、中国智慧、中国方案的优秀文化主体图书,打造新时代国际出版品牌。加强对外译介,以融通中外的语言、优秀的翻译作品讲好中国故事。

密切人文交往,打造国际交流对话平台。高度重视人际传播作用,完善各类文化传播机制性平台,结合高访外交、区域合作机制、公共外交等,扩大和深化文化交流。围绕治国理政与全球治理、人文对话、青年交流等重点,打造有影响力的国际交流对话平台。办好国际文化交流奖项评选。面向青少年开展知识分享和传播。加强双多边人文合作,不断丰富交流内容,拓展合作渠道等方式,全方位提升中华文化传播力影响力。

王学斌（中央党校文史部中国史教研室主任）：三个方面着力继续推进"第二个结合"研究

由新华社高端智库研究出品的《改变中国的"第二个结合"》，紧扣党的理论创新、制度创新最新动向，非常具有理论敏锐性、现实指导性。未来针对"第二个结合"的探讨，大致还有如下几个攻关重点与难点。

一是要系统梳理"第二个结合"的历史过程。"第二个结合"已经走过百年的历程，从1921年的初步结合到1943年5月份中共中央关于共产国际执委主席团提议解散共产国际决定中指出，要使得马克思主义、列宁主义这一革命科学更进一步的和中国革命实践、中国历史、中国文化争相结合起来；再到2021年的3月24日总书记在福建考察时强调，要把坚持马克思主义同弘扬中华优秀传统文化有机结合起来；我们会发现三个阶段，初步结合、争相结合、有机结合。我认为这个非常重要，对我们来说是一个提示，也就是说我们的结合实际上是有一个过程的。

随着我们对基本原理的领悟越来越深，对传统文化的把握越来越准，"第二个结合"就越来越彰显出理论的光芒和文明的底蕴，必将走向一个更为深刻的融合之境。

二是要深入全面把握中华文明，为人类文明新形态提供理论支撑。在"第二个结合"过程中，有五个方面的工作需要再展开：

第一，推动中华文明探源等一系列工程取得更加深刻的成果。

第二，深化研究我们文明的特质和形态，为人类文明新形态的理论建设提供重要的学理支撑。

第三，推动"两创"。正如报告中所指出，"两创"是桥梁和通道，没有这个路径不可能实现"第二个结合"。

第四，推动文明交流互鉴，向世界贡献更多关乎文明赓续的倡议。

第五，让宝贵的理论成果能够面向民间，让我们的文物、文化遗产、理论活起来，营造一种好的社会氛围。

三是要注重"第二个结合"内部逻辑的整体性和统一性。

"第二个结合"重大理论的内在逻辑要讲出来，战略立意要讲出来：

第一，"结合"的前提是彼此契合，彼此契合预示着结合主体的一种对等性。相互之间是可以，而且完全应该去结合的，这是对等的，而不是一种强势和弱势的关系问题。

第二，"结合"的结果是互相成就，就意味着"结合"结果的有机性。最后要形成一种新的有机的生命体，必然是有机的，必然是"你中有我、我中有你"，不可分割，也无可再分开的一个状态。

第三，"结合"筑牢了道路根基，指明了"结合"之于中国式现代化的重要性，一定是在我们不断推进、不断开拓、不断成就的过程中"结合"越来越成熟，道路越来越明晰。

第四，"第二个结合"又是一次思想解放，揭示了理论和制度创新的必然性。

第五，"结合"巩固了文化主体性，它毫无疑问进一步确证了习近平新时代中国特色社会主义思想之于强国复兴的一种决定性。

马克·力文（中央民族大学美籍教授、中国政府友谊奖获得者）：马克思主义加中国历史文化特征等于中国特色社会主义

卡尔·马克思和弗里德里希·恩格斯在其开创性著作《共产党宣言》当中指出，社会正处于不断变化的阶段，这是事实，一直都是事实，并将继续如此。对于整个世界各个国家以及其中的各种情况和现象来说都是如此。对于后来被称为马克思主义的、由马克思和恩格斯制定的理论原则也是如此。

马克思主义在中国得到了进一步的发展。正如毛泽东在1930年的文章《星星之火可以燎原》中提出，要建立农村革命根据地。这可以促进民族革命的高潮。换句话说，星星之火可以燎原，结合中国实际为中国革命创造了框架，取代了俄国革命依靠城市工人的模式，开辟了新的革命道路。

新华社的智库报告在第一章中第六点谈到了和谐的重要性，它指出中国始终坚持维护世界和平与共同发展的原则，给我印象深刻。中国致力于推动建设人类命运共同体，这是中国一直以来的传统,现在中国也在继续。

智库报告第二章讲述了中国的创新史。历史上中国有四大发明。报告提供了艺术创造力和"中国文化的审美精神和当代审美追求"的例子。显然,这仍然是现代中国的一个特征。

马克思主义的成功应用,总是需要与特定的传统文化以及特定国家的具体情况相结合的。用毛泽东的话说马克思主义不能在真空当中进行。这一点过去和现在都是正确的,无论社会主义发展到什么程度。就中国而言,这就是中国特色的社会主义。

安娜·马林博格－乌伊(菲律宾"亚洲世纪"战略研究所副所长):中国是发展中世界的光辉榜样

经过一个多世纪的政治发展,经济的进步和社会进步,拥有9800多万党员的中国共产党正焕发出更大的活力。

当我第一次听到人类命运共同体、合作共赢这样的词或者概念的时候,我脑海当中浮现的第一词就是团结。中国与全球南方国家的国际发展合作以及植根于中国历史经验、独立主权、身份、文化、独特价值观和传统的发展和现代化道路,所有的这些一直是发展中国家的灵感和发展的指南。

明竺(巴基斯坦学者、清华大学研究员):中国的经验对于发展中国家非常有借鉴意义

中国发展给我的激励就是对于自我的研究。我们要确定长期的一个愿景，但同时我们也要建立短期的目标，我认为这是非常重要的。

在这个报告中，已经谈到了我们要有各种不同的方法：第一，我们要有自信，理论和实践应该进行紧密的结合。第二，要解决全球的发展过程中不平等的现象。第三，中国的成功是建立在马克思主义原则和"第二个结合"的基础之上的，马克思主义已经变成了一种中国的文化。第四，中国不仅是帮助南方国家在发展，同时也在北方和南方国家之间进行沟通。第五，中国等一些国家的发展历程之所以是成功的，在于我们可以求同存异。我们只有了解差异，并且敬畏和尊重差异，才会对自己区域当中的独特历史感到自豪和自信。这种独特性和统一性我们是要共同平等地来进行培养的。

知所从来　方明所往

大道之源

Root to Success:
The Second Integration That Transforms China

改变中国的"第二个结合"

新华通讯社 出品　20'X3　4K

知所从来 方明所往

大道之源
改变中国的"第二个结合"

文化根魂
The Root of Culture

中华民族在几千年历史中创造和延续的中华优秀传统文化，是中华民族的根和魂。

新华通讯社 出品

20'X3 4K

新华社大型纪录片
《大道之源：改变中国的「第二个结合」》之《文化根魂》

第一集

文化根魂

【字幕】2021年7月1日，在庆祝中国共产党成立100周年大会上的重要讲话中，习近平总书记提出，把马克思主义基本原理"同中华优秀传统文化相结合"，即"第二个结合"。

【字幕】2023年6月2日，在文化传承发展座谈会上，习近平总书记说："把马克思主义基本原理同中国具体实际、同中华优秀传统文化相结合是必由之路。"

【总片名】大道之源：改变中国的"第二个结合"

【字幕】北京·中国国家版本馆中央总馆

【解说】燕山脚下，国家级文化殿堂俯瞰京华。

1600万余册纵贯千年的各类典籍版本汇聚于此，集纳先贤智慧，赓续中华文脉。

【字幕】北京·中国历史研究院

【解说】北京中轴线北延长线上，一条"历史大道"，连通古今，铭刻中华文明悠久历史。

2023年6月，习近平总书记专程到中国国家版本馆中央总馆和中国历史研究院考察调研，出席文化传承发展座谈会。

【解说+字幕】听取大家发言后，习近平总书记说：

在新的起点上继续推动文化繁荣、建设文化强国、建设中华民族现代文明，是我们在新时代新的文化使命。

【一】

【字幕】河北·正定

【解说】1600多年前，正定建城。

古人把对生活的美好憧憬赋予这片土地，南城门取名"长乐"，北城门叫作"永安"。

【字幕】"地当河朔称雄镇，虎踞龙盘燕赵间。" 清·容丕华

【解说】1982年，习近平到正定任职。这里源远流长的历史、深厚的文化底蕴，深深吸引着他。

【解说】隆兴寺位列中国十大名寺，是研究宋代建筑、造像、雕刻艺术的珍贵实物遗存。

【字幕】圣主本命长生祝延碑　宋末元初·赵孟頫

【解说】这块元代石碑，碑文由书法家赵孟頫书写。笔锋苍劲成熟，在书法艺术史上举足轻重。

【同期】时任河北正定县委办公室副主任 王志敏：他到隆兴寺，他发现了这个碑，根本没有任何保护，就躺在地上。风化、雨淋、日晒，有的字体就模糊了。

时任河北正定县委办公室副主任 朱博华：他就从心里疼这个碑，有感情。他说这不行，这是一个很好的碑。

【解说】习近平当即找到主管领导，提出严肃批评："我们保管不好文物，就是罪人，就会愧对后人。"

正定古城不到10平方公里内，有10个国家级文保单位。上世纪80年代初，许多文物都已历尽风霜、伤痕累累。

【同期】时任河北正定县委办公室干事 张银耀：因为正定遍地都是文物，老百姓也好，有些干部也好，好多拿它不当事。

时任河北正定县委办公室副主任 王志敏：财政收入都有限，筹款比较难。

【解说】面对困难，习近平态度坚决。他说："这些可都是国宝啊！一旦消失，就永远看不到了。我们保护和修复文物，既是对祖先负责，也是对后人负责。"

1984年，习近平向上级争取到一笔古建筑修缮专款。利用这笔资金，正定对隆兴寺大规模修缮，包括赵孟頫书法碑在内的许多块古碑得到妥善保护。

在正定工作期间，习近平身体力行推动文物保护工作，他健全保护制度、组织文物普查、修复古寺古碑……

今天的正定，登得上城楼，望得见古塔，记得住乡愁。千年古郡,见证着习近平对中华优秀传统文化的深沉热爱。

人们一直记得他在正定工作时写下的一句话:

【解说+字幕】一个热爱中华大地的人,他一定会爱她的每一条溪流,每一寸土地,每一页光辉的历史。

【二】

【字幕】2012年11月15日 北京

【解说】2012年11月15日,习近平当选中共中央总书记。

【同期】习近平:我们一定不负重托,不辱使命。

【解说】面对十多亿人的期望,习近平总书记重任在肩。如何在新的起点上,推进实现中华民族伟大复兴?在宏阔的时空维度,他不断探寻中华文明生生不息的密码。

【字幕】山东·曲阜

【解说+字幕】"有朋自远方来,不亦乐乎?" 春秋·《论语》

【解说】曲阜,是孔子的故乡。

2013年11月,习近平总书记来到曲阜考察。

【纪实】习近平:我到这里来,专门安排到曲阜,安排到孔府看一看,到孔子研究院看一看,就是要体现中央高度重视弘扬我们的传统文化。

【同期】孔子研究院原院长 杨朝明:专家学者座谈会,给我们留下很深的印象。从文化自知到文化自信,我觉得这就是中国道路，这就是中国特色的道路。

【解说＋字幕】习近平总书记说：

一个国家、一个民族的强盛，总是以文化兴盛为支撑的，中华民族伟大复兴需要以中华文化发展繁荣为条件。

【解说】当我们踏上第二个百年奋斗目标新征程，中国如何实现精神上的独立自主？在中国共产党百年华诞之际，习近平总书记给出坚定回答：

【同期】习近平：坚持把马克思主义基本原理同中国具体实际相结合、同中华优秀传统文化相结合。

【解说】"第二个结合"让我们在更广阔的文化空间中，充分利用中华优秀传统文化的宝贵资源，探索面向未来的理论和制度创新。

【三】

【解说】什么是传统文化？是我们背过的古诗，我们的姓氏，是我们吃的元宵汤圆，穿的苏杭丝绸，是我们看待世界的方式，日用而不觉。

【字幕】湖南·长沙

【解说】龙兵，湖南大学的一名思政课教师，他的职责是要让年轻的大学生树立正确的人生观。

【纪实】湖南大学马克思主义学院院长 龙兵：同学们好，今天我们与同学们交流的主题是以中国式现代化推进中华民族

改变中国的"第二个结合" ● 建设中华民族现代文明的理论创新与实践

伟大复兴的制度保障……

【同期】湖南大学马克思主义学院院长 龙兵：如何上好思政课，一直是我们思考的一个问题。让我们的思政课成为学生真心喜爱、终身受益、毕生难忘的课程。

【解说】为了让思政课教学更好地入脑入心，龙兵和同事们带着学生走出教室，走进广阔的社会课堂。

【同期】湖南大学马克思主义学院院长 龙兵：把我们中华优秀传统文化里面的人文精神运用到我们的思政课教学之中，让我们的学生到现场来体会，现场来感受，马克思主义中国化的内在道理。

【解说】龙兵没有想到，习近平总书记有一天会走进他的思政课堂。

2020年9月17日，习近平总书记来到湖南大学岳麓书院。

【纪实】习近平：岳麓书院一直是我有牵挂，这个学院在我们的传统文化中的地位、影响，我还是很有感触的。

【解说】岳麓书院是中国古代四大书院之一，育人千年，弦歌不绝，培养了一代又一代"以天下为己任"的经世济民之才。

在书院中心讲堂前，悬挂着一块"实事求是"的匾额。

【解说+字幕】"修学好古、实事求是。" 东汉·班固

【解说】1917年，岳麓书院将《汉书》中这句古人求索的箴言悬挂于讲堂作为校训。青年毛泽东曾寄住在岳麓书院，他常在此流连，思索"改造中国和世界"的方法。

习近平总书记仰望匾额、久久凝思。马克思主义和中华优秀传统文化来源不同，但彼此存在高度的契合性，相互契合才能有机结合。他说，

【解说+字幕】这里面的道路一定要搞清楚，一定要把真理本土化。

【解说】马克思主义只有中国化才能在中国大地上闪耀真理的光芒。

【纪实】习近平：这是一个英雄辈出的时代，你们这个年纪正当其时，形成成熟的人生观、价值观，走好人生的路。

【解说+字幕】在岳麓书院，习近平总书记说：

我们要坚定道路自信、理论自信、制度自信、文化自信，其中文化自信是更基础、更广泛、更深厚的自信。

【四】

【解说】带着对文化自信的深沉思索，习近平总书记步履不停。他说，中华文明博大精深、源远流长，是由各民族优秀文化百川汇流而成。

【字幕】新疆·乌恰

【解说】新疆帕米尔高原，中国版图的最西端。这里群山起伏，逶迤连绵，生活着古老的游牧民族——柯尔克孜族。

速度、力量、激情，骑马叼羊是勇敢者的游戏。关于叼羊运动的起源，有一种说法是来自《玛纳斯》的传说。

《玛纳斯》是世界级非物质文化遗产。一部23.6万行的民族史诗，描绘了柯尔克孜族社会生活的方方面面。

在草原上生活了五十多年，江努日最快乐的童年记忆，是跟爷爷学唱《玛纳斯》，讲述马背上英雄的故事。

【同期】《玛纳斯》非物质文化遗产传承人 江努日·图日干巴依：星期六下午放学的时候，放学后到爷爷那儿，爷爷叫我去赶牛羊，然后我就说你给我唱一段《玛纳斯》我再过去。

【解说】在英雄的世界里，一日千里。江努日唱着心爱的《玛纳斯》，走遍了家乡的山山水水，他成为家喻户晓的《玛纳斯》歌手。2019年，江努日被评为新疆维吾尔自治区级非遗传承人。

【字幕】新疆·乌鲁木齐

【解说】2022年，习近平总书记来到新疆考察。江努日带着徒弟们向总书记展示了一段《玛纳斯》。

总书记笑着问他，"可以唱多久？"

江努日说："一天一夜都唱不完。"

【纪实】习近平：《江格尔》《格萨尔王》《玛纳斯》，这都是我们少数民族的宝贵财富，也是我们中华民族的文化宝库中的宝贵财富。

【同期】《玛纳斯》非物质文化遗产传承人 江努日·图日干巴依：总书记问我有什么梦想，我的梦想是把《玛纳斯》不仅唱给国内的各族群众，还要唱给全世界，让全世界知道《玛纳斯》。

【解说】在习近平总书记的关心下,《玛纳斯》的传承方式更加丰富。小学课堂里,孩子们弹起库姆孜,学唱《玛纳斯》。新疆已经成立了《玛纳斯》研究中心。史诗的 8 部唱本实录整理出版,并翻译成多种语言走向世界。

从西陲边疆到北京故宫,从安阳殷墟到敦煌莫高窟……习近平总书记的文化足迹遍及全国。泱泱中华,文明博大,习近平总书记深刻阐释了中华文明的五个特性:

【解说+字幕】中华文明具有突出的连续性、创新性、统一性、包容性、和平性。

【五】

【字幕】陕西·西安

【解说】晨钟暮鼓、汉风唐韵。西安,处处流露出千年古都的包容自信。

全长 13.74 公里,西安城墙是中国现存规模最宏大、保存最完整的古代城垣建筑。它穿越古今,传承着城市的历史记忆。

习近平总书记对西安城墙有特殊的感情。2015 年,春节将至,习近平总书记来到西安,登上城墙,考察城墙保护状况。他说:"这是世界级的宝贝,要保护传承好。"

【纪实】《梦长安》演出

"恭迎八方宾客莅临长安"

【解说】3 个月后,古城西安用一场盛唐气派的入城仪式迎接远道而来的宾客。习近平总书记同外宾共同观看了文艺演出《梦长安》。

【纪实】《梦长安》演出

【解说】在历史文化与现代舞台结合的光影盛宴中,"穿越"历史,重回大唐。

【同期】西安曲江城墙旅游发展有限公司副总经理 陈朋:在城墙文物载体上面去做这种迎宾仪式,这是在全世界应该是独一份的。

【解说】如何推动文化复兴?习近平总书记身体力行,探寻中华文化守正创新之路。

2017年10月,他在党的十九大报告中提出了更高的要求。

【同期】习近平:坚持创造性转化、创新性发展,不断铸就中华文化新辉煌。

【解说】推动中华文明创造性转化、创新性发展,全民族文化创新活力竞相迸发。用文化激活城市建设,成了西安新的目标。

大雁塔下,有一条两公里长的景观大道,名叫"大唐不夜城"。虽然地处核心,但商业街的定位限制了它的发展。

【同期】西安曲江文化旅游股份有限公司总经理 谢晓宁:在2018年以前,其实大唐不夜城这条街区它是通车的,街上静的时候它就只有一万人,对唐文化有什么感受,很少。

【解说】2018年,大唐不夜城迎来升级改造。

【同期】西安曲江文化旅游股份有限公司演艺中心原总经理 苏卉：我们都是以这种中国传统文化、历史文化去转换成演艺，把中国这种传统文化用这种现代的手法去表达。

【解说】夜幕降临，唐朝的簪花仕女，穿越到现代游园；胡旋舞的造型来自莫高窟的壁画；站上骆驼载乐俑，跳起千年的舞步。大唐不夜城的客流量从当初的每天一万人增长到三四十万。

【解说】2020年，习近平总书记到西安考察调研。行程的最后一站，是大唐不夜城。

【纪实】店主：您尝一个家乡的味道吧。

店主：您到我们这儿来转转吧。唐装、华服。

习近平：穿的这个是唐装还是华服？

店主：唐装。

习近平：越来越多的人穿唐装。

【解说】2023年5月，习近平总书记再次在这里主持主场外交活动，迎接中亚五国元首。

【字幕+同期】"长安复携手，再顾重千金" 唐·李白

【同期】习近平：今天我们在西安相聚，续写千年友情，开辟崭新未来，具有十分重要的意义。

【解说】在习近平总书记引领推动下，中华优秀传统文化的"一池春水"被彻底激活，文明古国阔步迈向文化强国。

【解说】把马克思主义基本原理同中华优秀传统文化相结

合，是习近平总书记面对时代之问的郑重回答。

【解说】从文物保护，到文化传承，从文化自信，到文明复兴。

【字幕】"大道之行、天下为公"

"礼序乾坤、乐和天地"

"民为邦本、为政以德"

"自强不息、厚德载物"

"文以载道、以文化人"

"讲信修睦、亲仁善邻"

【解说】他将信仰信念与中华民族千年理想有机结合，将制度成熟定型与礼乐文明有机结合，将发展思想与民本思想有机结合，将核心价值与传统取向有机结合，将社会主义先进文化与中华优秀传统文化有机结合，将命运与共与协和万邦有机结合。

这是又一次思想解放。

他以真理力量激活古老文明，以文化之火照亮复兴之路。让今天的中国，面向未来，自信前行。

知所从来 方明所往

大道之源
改变中国的"第二个结合"

治理智慧
The Wisdom of Governance

中华民族有着五千多年悠久文明历史的深厚底蕴，我们带领人民走的是中国特色社会主义道路。

新华通讯社 出品
20'X3 4K

新华社大型纪录片
《大道之源：改变中国的「第二个结合」》之《治理智慧》

第二集

治理智慧

【字幕】2021年7月1日,在庆祝中国共产党成立100周年大会上的重要讲话中,习近平总书记提出,把马克思主义基本原理"同中华优秀传统文化相结合",即"第二个结合"。

【字幕】2023年6月2日,在文化传承发展座谈会上,习近平总书记说:"把马克思主义基本原理同中国具体实际、同中华优秀传统文化相结合是必由之路。"

【总片名】大道之源:改变中国的"第二个结合"

【字幕】四川·三苏祠

【解说】时光流转,古祠悠悠。

苏洵、苏轼、苏辙,一门三父子位列唐宋八大家,绝无仅有。

中华文化在岁月中薪火相传,跨越千年依旧生机盎然。先贤智慧怎样启迪新时代的哲思?

【解说】2022年6月,习近平总书记来到三苏祠。观照古今,他的答案清晰而坚定:

【字幕】中华民族有着五千多年悠久文明历史的深厚底蕴,我们带领人民走的是中国特色社会主义道路。要善于从中华优秀传统文化中汲取治国理政的理念和思维。

【一】

【字幕】青海·海南藏族自治州贵德县尕让乡

【解说】初夏清晨,仁欠多杰整理羊群,动身前往附近的草场。羊群,是一家人生计所系。这片山水,维系着多杰家生活的全部。

【同期】贵德县尕让乡东果堂村村民 仁欠多杰:以前在我们这个村庄里面,住户也多羊也多,羊多的话草也吃不上,吃不上草羊就不长膘,卖不出好价钱。

【解说】过度放牧、草场退化、牲畜减产。2017年,多杰家被识别为建档立卡贫困户。

【解说】多杰的家乡,地处青藏高原。2.8亿年前,这里是一片海。亿万年间,沧桑巨变。海水化成了青海瞬息万变的云、纯洁神圣的雪。

长江、黄河、澜沧江从此发源,青海因此被誉为"中华水塔",是中国重要的水源涵养地和生态安全屏障。

【解说】受气候变化和人为活动影响,青海的生态一度退化,草原面积减少，水土流失严重。

【解说】"中华水塔"的安危，习近平总书记始终牵挂。2016年8月，他来到青海，走进青海省生态环境监测中心，通过视频连线，详细询问三江源的生态资源管护工作。

【同期】习近平：生态保护这是国家的一个战略性的考虑，中国要发展，我们一定要把生态文明建设搞上去。

【解说+字幕】"万物各得其和以生，各得其养以成" 战国·荀子

【解说】遵循总书记的嘱托，改变生态面貌，成为青海的首要任务。

为全方位监测环境，生态环境监测中心增加观测点位，配合实时传输网络，打造生态环境监管的"千里眼"；省内九成以上国土面积规划为限制开发区和禁止开发区；85%的野生动物栖息地纳入自然保护地管理；青海设置各类生态保护公益岗位超过14万个，每年为农牧民增收约10亿元。

2020年，多杰有了一个新身份，江拉林场生态管护员。家乡的生态，正在一天天变好。

【解说】2021年全国两会，青海代表团审议现场，有一位代表拿出照片，请坐在对面的习近平总书记观看。

【同期】全国人大代表 孔庆菊：一个就是我们的雪豹，就在我们的河滩出现了，这个是荒漠猫，它们都是我们国家重点的一级保护动物。

【解说】总书记说,大家的生态保护意识也增强了,看到了生态本身的经济价值。

【解说】3个月后,习近平总书记再次来到青海。

【同期】习近平:把青海的生态建设好、生态资源保护好,这也是我们的宝藏,是资源,也是财富。

【解说】"天人合一、万物并育",是中华民族的自然观,也是辩证统一的智慧。早在主政浙江期间,习近平就重视环境保护和经济发展的关系。

【同期】习近平:绿水青山就是金山银山。

【解说】党的十八大以来,随着这一生态思想日益深入人心,人们越来越能感受到其中传承千年的中国智慧。

【解说+字幕】"天育物有时、地生财有限。"生态环境没有替代品,用之不觉,失之难存。

【二】

【解说】以史鉴今,资政治国。从中华优秀传统文化中汲取智慧,是习近平总书记一直秉持的治理理念。

主政浙江期间,他曾经用全局思维,推动了宁波、舟山两港的合并。

【字幕】浙江·宁波

【解说】今年43岁的竺士杰,是一名土生土长的宁波人。

【同期】宁波舟山港集团北三集司桥吊班大班长 竺士杰:

我小时候就住在甬江口边上,所以我小的时候就是听着轮船的汽笛声长大的。

【解说】每天清晨,竺士杰都要前往海边港区。他是一名桥吊司机,工作地是一座年货物吞吐量超过 10 亿吨的世界级大港,宁波舟山港。

【解说】但在 2002 年,宁波、舟山却分别拥有各自的港口,即便两港货物吞吐量相加,距离世界级港口仍有很大差距。

两个港口虽然近在咫尺,属于同一经济腹地,位于同一海域,使用同一航道,但在管理运营上,却相互分割,发展瓶颈日益凸显。

【同期】原宁波港集团总裁 李令红:宁波方面的优势,就是有码头管理的经验。但是岸线已经不够了,大量的深水岸线都在舟山。

【字幕】浙江·舟山市

【解说】舟山,号称千岛之城。与宁波隔海相望,虽然有丰富的岸线资源,但优势难以充分施展。

【解说】2002 年底,习近平主政浙江。在深入调研后,他重新审视浙江资源禀赋,提出宁波、舟山两港整合,一体发展。这项工作的关键,就是将舟山和内地跨海相连。

在他的推动下,总长度 48.16 公里的五座跨海大桥飞架南北东西,不仅连接起舟山、宁波等地,更迅速激发出山海协作优势,让宁波、舟山两港合并水到渠成。

【解说】2005年12月,宁波－舟山港管理委员会正式挂牌,迈出了建成世界大港的第一步。

【同期】习近平:今后的大手笔建设,一个浓墨重彩之处,将是在港口建设方面。港口建设的重点,将是在宁波、舟山一体化之举。

【解说】日益增加的港口吞吐量,将竺士杰锻炼成技能标兵,他创下每小时起吊185个集装箱的世界纪录。

【同期】宁波舟山港集团北三集司桥吊班大班长 竺士杰:习近平总书记说,你们一体化以后,集装箱吞吐量完成700万箱,他还会来参加我们的仪式,结果在当年我们就完成700万箱了,所以习近平总书记如约而至。

【解说】2008年,宁波舟山港建成首个30万吨级深水航道;2009年,年货物吞吐量跃升至世界第一;2018年,年集装箱吞吐量首次突破2500万标准箱。

【解说】2020年3月29日,习近平总书记又一次来到宁波舟山港,冒雨察看码头现场集装箱作业场景。竺士杰作为代表向总书记汇报工作。

【同期】宁波舟山港集团北三集司桥吊班大班长 竺士杰:一直有一种觉得很幸运的感觉,整个港口给我们员工的感受就是一直在高速发展,一直在蓬勃地发展。

【解说】今天的宁波舟山港,是一座拥有19个港区,超过200座万吨级以上大型泊位,年货物吞吐量连续14年位居全球第一的超级大港。

【解说+字幕】"不谋全局者,不足谋一域" 清·陈澹然

【解说】党的十八大以来,随着全面深化改革稳步推进,京津冀协同发展、长江经济带发展、粤港澳大湾区建设先后布局,透过这些举措,人们看到了习近平总书记从中华优秀传统文化中汲取的治理智慧。

【解说+字幕】处理好局部和全局,当前和长远,重点和非重点的关系,在权衡利弊中趋利避害,作出最为有利的战略抉择。

【三】

【解说】对于习近平总书记而言,要下好新时代的全国一盘棋,必须迎接一系列重大挑战。

2012年,中国仍有近一亿绝对贫困人口。习近平总书记接过了中国几代人接续奋斗的减贫任务。"致广大而尽精微。"

精准扶贫,成为行动指南。

【同期】习近平:抓扶贫的时候切忌喊大口号,实事求是、因地制宜、分类指导、精准扶贫。

【字幕】贵州·新仁苗族乡

【解说】乌江上游,六冲河畔。群山之中的新仁苗族乡,是杨文丽出生的地方。

【同期】贵州省黔西市新仁苗族乡化屋村村民 杨文丽:小

的时候没有被子盖，脚底下放一个瓶子装温水（取暖）。村里面看到的都是小孩子和老人。

【解说】2016年，在精准扶贫政策推动下，村民们搬下大山。杨文丽在移民安置点创办刺绣生产合作社。几十名村民在家门口找到了工作。600多平方米的车间内，每年生产3000多套苗族服饰，通过直播卖到全国各地。

【同期】贵州省黔西市新仁苗族乡化屋村村民 杨文丽：我们是从小就要学习刺绣的，世世代代都这样。

【解说】在苗绣中，每个图腾都有独特的含义，龙代表自然，树象征生命。杨文丽现在经常绣下蝴蝶，表达对幸福的向往。

【解说】2021年春节前夕，习近平总书记来到化屋村，走进杨文丽的车间。

【同期】习近平：传统的也是时尚的，既是文化又是产业，它既是能够弘扬民族文化、传统文化，用产业来扶贫，用产业来振兴乡村，又可以作出贡献。

【解说】"天下大事，必作于细。"春秋·老子

苗家绣娘用一针一线绣出了新的生活。

打赢脱贫攻坚战，精准是制胜秘诀。习近平总书记特别强调工作中的绣花功夫，他说。

【解说＋字幕】要强化精准思维，做到谋划时统揽大局、操作中细致精当，以绣花功夫把工作做扎实、做到位。

【四】

【字幕】湖北·武汉

【解说】大江大湖的滋养,塑造了武汉天生的豪情。
"敢为天下先",武汉人的性格与这座城市不谋而合。

【解说】2013年7月,习近平总书记来到武汉东湖高新区考察。这是首批国家级高新区,它还有一个被人熟知的名字,中国光谷。

【解说+字幕】"不日新者必日退"。(北宋程颢、程颐《二程集·河南程氏遗书·卷第二十五》)

【解说】革故鼎新的思想方法,贯穿习近平总书记治国理政的全过程。科技创新,一直被他摆在国家发展全局的核心位置。

在光谷展示中心,总书记详细观看了创新成果展示,语重心长地提出希望。

【同期】习近平:工业要靠自力更生、自主研发、自主创新,形成我们的核心竞争力。

【解说】习近平总书记的嘱托,成为光谷科技工作者的行动指南。

邓家科,高级工程师,在业内被称为中国激光行业的"见证人"。

【解说】激光,20世纪以来继原子能、计算机、半导体之后,人类又一重大发明。"最亮的光、最准的尺、最快的刀",

激光的应用，将人类制造业推进快车道。小到手表手机，大到飞机轮船，激光在制造业中的参与程度，决定着一个国家工业体系的实力。

但在二十多年前，从激光光源到应用技术，几乎全被国外垄断。

【同期】华工激光总经理 邓家科：因为那个时候激光切割机都是靠进口，你买到的可能还是他淘汰的东西，你真正要买的最先进的他有可能还不卖。

【解说】那时，高速发展的中国汽车制造业，对车身激光焊接切割技术提出了迫切需求。这对华工激光，既是机遇，更是挑战。

【同期】华工激光总经理 邓家科：国家对我们大量的资金的投入，同时还有政策方面的一些引导。就是国家支持你，这样的话创新就会有保障。

【解说】在政策支持下，他们自主研发的车身激光焊接切割技术通过反复试验论证，获得国家科技进步一等奖。2016年初，习近平总书记在人民大会堂为科研团队颁奖。

【同期】华工激光总经理 邓家科：特别是最近这十年，我们通过追赶国外的一些先进技术，到跟国外的一些技术同步，现在我们基本上在某些方面已经在领跑这个行业的发展。

【解说】习近平总书记对于科技创新的强调，始终激励着华工激光，在车身激光焊接切割技术以外，他们还创造了多项国内行业第一，牵头制定了中国激光行业首个国际标准。

【解说】2022年6月，习近平总书记再次来到光谷，走进华工激光考察。在车间大楼前，他说，"把科技的命脉掌握在自己手中，国家才能真正强大起来。"

【解说】习近平总书记的期望，正在一天天变为现实。今天的中国光谷，已经成为代表国家参与全球光电子信息产业竞争与合作的"主力军"。

在广阔的中华大地上，光谷只是一个缩影。党的十八大以来，中国成功进入创新型国家行列，不断创造着新的可能。

【解说+字幕】"观之上古，验之当世。" 西汉·贾谊

【解说】思想之意义，在于应历史之变、解时代之问。

中国文化、中国智慧、中国精神，浸润在习近平总书记治国理政的方方面面。

【同期】习近平：只有把马克思主义基本原理同中国具体实际相结合，同中华优秀传统文化相结合，坚持运用辩证唯物主义和历史唯物主义，才能正确回答时代和实践提出的重大问题，才能始终保持马克思主义的蓬勃生机和旺盛活力。

【解说】以"中国之制"推进"中国之治"，中国式现代化的道路，越走越宽广。

知 所 从 来　方 明 所 往

大道之源
改变中国的"第二个结合"

文明之光
The Light of Civilization

对历史最好的继承，就是创造新的历史；
对人类文明最大的礼敬，就是创造人类文明新形态。

新华通讯社 出品
20'X3 4K

新华社大型纪录片
《大道之源：改变中国的『第二个结合』》之《文明之光》

第三集

文明之光

【字幕】2021年7月1日,在庆祝中国共产党成立100周年大会上的重要讲话中,习近平总书记提出,把马克思主义基本原理同中华优秀传统文化相结合,即"第二个结合"。

【字幕】2023年6月2日,在文化传承发展座谈会上,习近平总书记说:"把马克思主义基本原理同中国具体实际、同中华优秀传统文化相结合是必由之路。"

【总片名】大道之源 改变中国的第二个结合

【解说】法国尼斯,地中海沿岸最迷人的城市之一。

作为世界文化名城,多种文化不断在此碰撞、交融。

【解说】2019年3月24日,正在法国访问的习近平主席在尼斯收到一份特殊礼物——1688年出版的首部《论语导读》法文版著作。

《论语导读》跟随习近平主席不远万里回到中国，跨越几个世纪的中西文化交流，让文明之光交相辉映。

习近平总书记曾这样说，

【解说+字幕】中华民族具有5000多年连绵不断的文明历史，创造了博大精深的中华文化，为人类文明进步作出了不可磨灭的贡献。

【一】

【字幕】福建·武夷山

【解说】发源于武夷山脉主峰，这条溪流逶迤百里，穿山而来。千峰秀色，九折成带。

【解说+字幕】"问渠那得清如许？为有源头活水来"宋·朱熹

【解说】南宋思想家朱熹徜徉九曲溪畔，写下这样的诗句。

【解说】隐居在武夷山近50年，朱熹著书立说、倡道讲学。

【同期】武夷山市政府四级调研员 周洪舰：朱熹坚守儒家思想这条主线，承上启下，继往开来。

【解说】1999年12月，武夷山被联合国教科文组织列入世界自然与文化遗产名录。时任福建省代省长的习近平专门致信祝贺。

【解说】2002年初，中国社会科学院致函福建省，建议在武夷山设立宋明理学研究中心。习近平批示要求办好，并拨款支持。

【同期】时任武夷山市副市长 阮雪清：我们拨了50亩地，在武夷学院里面盖。他第一个支持的就是这个。

【解说】2005年，在习近平的关心推动下，宋明理学研究中心正式挂牌。

在后来的日子里，研究中心承担了多个国家级社科课题研究，编辑出版学术类和普及性著作23部、1000多万字。

【解说】2021年3月，习近平总书记来到武夷山朱熹园。早年就同总书记相识的张建光，专门为总书记讲解，老朋友相见格外亲切。

【同期】福建省南平市朱子文化研究会名誉会长、福建省文史研究馆馆员 张建光：我跟总书记分别了20年，没想到一照面他就叫出我的名字。他碰到所有的游客都跟他们介绍，这里是武夷山，武夷山是"双世遗"，是中华民族的骄傲。

【解说】在展厅墙上，展示着朱熹民本思想语录，总书记在此驻足。他曾多次引用朱熹的话，诠释民心是最大的政治。

【同期】福建省南平市朱子文化研究会名誉会长、福建省文史研究馆馆员 张建光：朱子关于民本思想的这些方面，跟我们党是一致的。

武夷学院朱子学研究中心研究员、中国社会科学院哲学所宋明理学研究中心秘书长 张品端：以民为本，社稷为民而立。跟我们发展到现在提出以人民为中心，是一脉相承的。

【解说】相互契合，才能有机结合。在朱熹园，习近平总书记郑重地说：

【纪实】习近平：如果没有五千年文明，哪里有什么中国特色？如果不是中国特色，哪有我们现在这么成功的中国特色社会主义道路？

【解说】800多年前，朱熹亲手种下这棵古樟。今天依旧绿荫如盖。

习近平总书记说：

【解说+字幕】只有植根本国、本民族历史文化沃土，马克思主义真理之树才能根深叶茂。

【二】

【解说】领航14亿多人口的大国，习近平总书记曾这样说："我们从哪里来？我们走向何方？中国到了今天，我无时无刻不提醒自己，要有这样一种历史感。"

【字幕】上海·中共一大会址

【解说】党的十九大闭幕不久，习近平总书记沿着早期共产党人的足迹，探寻党的精神密码。

【同期】中共一大纪念馆宣传教育部主任 杨宇：我们都知道中共一大上其实当时通过了两个重要文件，一个是中国共产党的第一个纲领，一个是《关于当前实际工作的决议》。当时总书记一个人默默地在一大上通过的第一个纲领前逐字逐句地在看，细细地品读。

【解说】1921年，10多位有志之士，怀着对马克思主义的憧憬，在这里播下中国革命的火种。

习近平总书记说，我们党从这里诞生，从这里出征，从这里走向全国执政。这里是我们党的根脉。

【字幕】河南·安阳

【解说】不忘本来，才能开辟未来。

将马克思主义基本原理同中华优秀传统文化相结合，筑牢了道路根基，让中国特色社会主义道路有了更加宏阔深远的历史纵深。

【字幕】河南·殷墟

【解说】河南殷墟，中国考古发掘时间最长、面积最大的古代都城遗址。甲骨文、青铜器、宫殿等惊世发现，揭开了一个3000多年前璀璨王朝的神秘面纱。

在诸多考古发现中，甲骨文是重中之重。16万多片甲骨，约4500个单字，中国信史向上推进了约1000年。

【同期】中国社会科学院考古研究所研究员、安阳工作站副站长 何毓灵：我所理解的甲骨文，它的最大特点，它可以超越方言，超越语言性。这样就很大程度上解决了我们的什么样的问题？我们幅员广阔的中华大地上文化的交流的问题。从甲骨文之后的3000多年，不管王朝怎么变化，以甲骨文为代表的汉字始终是我们中华文化的载体。

【解说】一笔一画，一撇一捺。汉字承载着中华文明的基因密码。

【解说】习近平总书记十分关心甲骨文的保护研究。2019年，他致信祝贺甲骨文发现和研究120周年，寄语广大相关领域研究人员："新形势下，要确保甲骨文等古文字研究有人做、有传承。"

【解说】2020年9月，中共中央政治局就我国考古最新发现及其意义为题举行第二十三次集体学习。

总书记指出："更好认识源远流长、博大精深的中华文明，为弘扬中华优秀传统文化、增强文化自信提供坚强支撑"。

【同期】中华文明探源工程首席专家、中国考古学会理事长 王巍：我们也通过学习，我们也了解总书记那么高度地重视考古，就是因为它能够揭示我们的文明，文明的历程、文明的辉煌、文明对人类的贡献。这个用总书记的话说，增强做中国人的志气、骨气和底气。

【解说】2022年10月28日，习近平总书记来到河南安阳，考察殷墟遗址。他仔细观摩青铜器、玉器、甲骨文等出土文物，感慨地说："殷墟我向往已久"。中华优秀传统文化是我们党创新理论的"根"，我们推进马克思主义中国化时代化的根本途径是"两个结合"。

【同期】河南省安阳市文物局党组书记、局长 李晓阳：殷墟作为中国考古学圣地，以考古学的方法和理论来构建我们的古史，我觉得也是总书记重视殷墟的一个很重要的方面。

【解说】在殷墟的考察中,习近平总书记深情地谈起这次考察的目的:

【解说+字幕】更深地学习理解中华文明,古为今用,为更好建设中华民族现代文明提供借鉴。

【三】

【字幕】海南·文昌

【新闻声】"今天上午,天舟六号货运飞船与长征七号遥七运载火箭组合体垂直转运至发射区。"

"这是天宫空间站投入正式运营后的首次发射任务。"

【字幕】2023年5月7日

天舟六号货运飞船发射任务

倒计时81小时

【纪实】文昌 01 报告

我是文昌 01 请讲

【解说】这是中国空间站全面建成后的首次货运飞行任务。

随着"第二个结合"理论逐步化作实践,今天的中国人正在携手创造属于这个时代的新文化,建设中华民族现代文明。

【纪实】宇亮,我们还是一级给你报氧氮加注准备的口令。

【解说】王宇亮是这次任务的 01 指挥员。

【同期】天舟六号货运飞船发射任务 01 指挥员 王宇亮:这个位置就相当于一个任务的大总管一样,就是要按照既定的任务工作程序有序地推进。

【字幕】天舟六号货运飞船发射任务

倒计时3小时

【解说】5月的文昌已进入雨季,降水和雷暴成为影响火箭发射的关键天气因素。

【同期】天舟六号货运飞船发射任务01指挥员 王宇亮:最大的困难的话就是到了(发)射前6分钟之后,基本上给大家商量讨论的时间就没那么多了。

【解说】6分钟,是发射前最关键的阶段。但中国人的飞天梦,已经延续数千年。

【解说+字幕】"不知天上宫阙,今夕是何年"宋·苏轼

【解说】从嫦娥奔月的神话到莫高窟的飞天,中国人从未放弃仰望星空,探索宇宙。

"祝融"探火、"嫦娥"奔月、"天宫"览胜……"天舟""神舟",一次次将人类的梦想运抵灿烂星河。

【解说】2022年4月,习近平总书记到文昌航天发射场视察。他依次来到航天器总装测试厂房和火箭水平测试、垂直总装测试厂房。

【同期】天舟六号货运飞船发射任务01指挥员 王宇亮:我和其余两百四十多名科技工作人员在这里见到了我们的总书记,也就是大概在这个位置。总书记对我们文昌发射场执行过的任务如数家珍。

改变中国的"第二个结合" —— 建设中华民族现代文明的理论创新与实践

【解说】在习近平总书记的持续关怀下,载人航天事业取得跨越式发展和历史性成就。文昌航天发射场也在航天梦的追寻路上大步向前。今天,它将再一次见证中国航天的高光时刻。

【字幕】天舟六号货运飞船发射任务

倒计时1小时

【同期】出镜记者:我们于晚上七点半抵达文昌发射场……

出镜记者:现在天舟六号货运飞船和长征七号遥七运载火箭……

出镜记者:已经完成了推进剂的加注……

【纪实】"5 4 3 2 1,点火"

"点火"

【解说】装载着中华民族飞天梦的火箭,又一次升空。

它点燃了每一个中国人的激情、骄傲和自信。正如习近平总书记深刻指出,

【解说+字幕】我们党领导人民不仅创造了世所罕见的经济快速发展和社会长期稳定两大奇迹,而且成功走出了中国式现代化道路,创造了人类文明新形态。

【四】

【字幕】英国·伦敦

【解说】"第二个结合"理论蕴含的世界观和方法论,也为破解世界难题提供了中国智慧、中国方案。

【解说】86岁的马丁·阿尔布劳是一名社会学家。过去的半个多世纪以来，他一直致力于全球化等国际议题的研究。在国际学术界，阿尔布劳被称为"全球化"概念的首创者。

【同期】英国社会学家 马丁·阿尔布劳：我致力于解决与人类社会、全球社会、全球化的未来有关的问题，我想为世界变得更美好作出贡献。

【解说】"全球化"概念提出后的20多年里，世界格局发生重大改变。阿尔布劳一直希望为他的研究找到新的视角。

2015年4月，《习近平谈治国理政》在伦敦发行。阿尔布劳受邀在会上致辞。这本书，让阿尔布劳第一次接触到习近平治国理政的思想理论。

【同期】英国社会学家 马丁·阿尔布劳：习近平的论述是极具体系架构的。中国有着灿烂辉煌文明史。而今天中国的复兴，正是被这些思想所驱动，这在当代世界是前所未有的。思想的重要性将中国带入了一个新时代。

【解说】发布会后，阿尔布劳开始了一个新的研究计划：他要以《习近平谈治国理政》一书为基础，研究中国和全球化。

2016年，阿尔布劳的研究项目开启。他开始学习中文，并阅读大量书籍。那年，他79岁。

习近平总书记曾多次引用过费孝通的那句话："美美与共，天下大同"。习近平的重要思想，成为阿尔布劳研究的重要依据。

【同期】英国社会学家 马丁·阿尔布劳：是他(费孝通)提出，

中国农民不仅从种植中获益,还能从为集体的贡献中获益。

【解说】2018年,阿尔布劳将研究成果写成了一本25万字的社会学著作《中国在人类命运共同体中的角色》。

2018年4月15日,在伦敦书展上,阿尔布劳的新书正式签约出版。

【纪实】英国社会学家 马丁·阿尔布劳:今天对我来说是个特殊的时刻。

【解说】这本书一共14章。阿尔布劳在书中写道,"中国为推动构建人类命运共同体所提出的'一带一路'倡议等公共产品为各国人民带来巨大机遇,中国在谋求自身发展的同时,始终致力于为世界人民谋福祉。"

【解说】"大道之行也,天下为公。"

习近平总书记用"天下一家"的思想推动共同发展,提出全球发展倡议。一大批有利于各国发展和惠及民生的项目在世界各地启动。一个个公路、铁路、桥梁、电站和港口项目,助力各国完善基础设施建设,打破发展瓶颈。

中国是联合国安理会常任理事国中派出维和人员最多的国家。习近平总书记用"协和万邦"的理念助力世界和平,提出全球安全倡议。

他用"和而不同"的胸襟倡导美美与共,提出全球文明倡议。一场场文明交融的盛会在中国举办,奏响友谊的华美乐章。

他引领新时代的中国携手世界,弘扬全人类共同价值,不断为人类文明百花园作出新的贡献。

【解说】"第二个结合"助推马克思主义中国化时代化实现新飞跃。习近平总书记在新时代文化建设方面的新思想新观点新论断，是新时代党领导文化建设实践经验的理论总结，丰富和发展了马克思主义文化理论，构成了习近平新时代中国特色社会主义思想的文化篇，形成了习近平文化思想。

思想之光，跨越时空、指引未来：

【字幕】对历史最好的继承，就是创造新的历史；

对人类文明最大的礼敬，就是创造人类文明新形态。

Introduction

"This ancient culture is suddenly full of vigor and strength. That's a mystery. No one could have imagined it!" exclaimed German political thinker Helmut Schmidt in a public interview when discussing Chinese culture.

With its super size and strong cohesiveness of society, China has achieved the remarkable "twin miracles" of fast economic growth and long-term social stability over the past few decades.

It is on the path of development and progress with safety and stability for its people. China's 5,000-year-old civilization and culture of more than 10,000 years have been developing with vigor and vitality. How can we explain China's success?

"Without China's 5,000-year-old civilization, where would the unique characteristics of China come from? And without the unique characteristics of China, where would our successful socialist path with Chinese characteristics be today?" Xi Jinping, general secretary of the Communist Party of China (CPC) Central Committee, said while paying an inspection visit to a park dedicated to Zhu Xi on Mount Wuyi in Fujian Province on March 22, 2021.

Zhang Jianguang, an expert on literature and history who guided Xi on the tour, said this revelation is simply amazing and will have far-reaching implications.[1]

Understanding the CPC is key to understanding today's China. Understanding China requires grasping the "cultural and civilizational soil" in which the CPC is firmly rooted.

In the history of the development of the CPC's theory, since the 1940s, there has been the accumulated practice of "integrating the basic tenets of Marxism with China's specific realities" with conscious summarization, which has successfully guided the CPC in leading the people's revolution, construction, and reform. Today's experts on the CPC's history call this practice the "First Integration." On July 1, 2021, in his speech at the gathering celebrating the 100th anniversary of the founding of the CPC, Xi Jinping formally put forward "integrating

---

[1] Interview with Zhang Jianguang, February 23, 2023.

the basic tenets of Marxism with fine traditional Chinese culture." His proposal has become known as the "Second Integration."

This innovative theory accurately grasps the current international and domestic trends, conforms to the historical process of the great rejuvenation of the Chinese nation, and demonstrates that since the 18th National Congress of the CPC, Chinese leaders have bravely stood at the forefront of the times with great vision and led China toward the great prospect of building a human community with a shared future. They have guided the Chinese people in strengthening their historical perspective, reinforcing their identity, and better interpreting the Chinese civilization, logically and coherently explaining China's governance today.

When attending the Symposium on Cultural Inheritance and Development in Beijing on June 2, 2023, Xi Jinping delivered an important speech, emphasizing, "Why is our socialism different? Why can it be full of vigor and vitality? The key lies in Chinese characteristics, and the key to Chinese characteristics lies in the 'Two Integrations'." "Integration is not a dish of assorted hors d'oeuvres. Neither is it a simple physical reaction. It is, however, a profound chemical reaction that creates an organically unified new cultural life."

This report argues that the "Second Integration" theory can be understood through six "organic integrations": the organic integration of communist and socialist beliefs with the millennial ideal of the Chinese nation, the organic integration of the matured and well-defined socialist system with Chinese characteristics with the ritual-and-music civilization, the organic integration of the people-centered idea of development with the people-oriented thought running through China for 5,000 years, the organic integration of core value of socialism with the traditional value orientation of the Chinese nation, the organic integration of the advanced socialist culture with fine traditional Chinese culture, and the organic integration of the concept of a human community with a shared future with the path of harmonious coexistence among nations.

The "Second Integration" theory, coming from the depths of Chinese history, has identified the points of convergence of Marxism with fine traditional Chinese culture, preserved the Chinese nation's roots and soul, activated the vitality of traditional culture, made a new great leap forward in adapting Marxism to the Chinese context, and created a new form of human civilization.

What is the scientific path to realizing the "Second Integration"? This report crystallizes it into the methodology of ten perspectives.

As a major country still growing considerably, China's conceptual changes and governance strategies are not only fundamentally changing China but will also have a profound impact on the world. The theory and practice of the "Second Integration" have shown the world that China's growth will continue to provide the world with the most significant public good of peaceful development and bring stability and certainty to the global community. Simultaneously, other countries can observe and use for reference China's experience of governance from the perspective of the "Second Integration."

The "Second Integration" has created a new pattern of the CPC's theoretical innovation and opened up a new realm of adapting Marxism to the Chinese context and the needs of our times. It is a key to understanding China in the new era, a pair of insightful eyes to observe Chinese modernization and a new form of human civilization, and a method to understand the relationship between China and the world.

It is China's new "cultural" way of governance leading the future in the 21st century.

- The "Second Integration" is another initiative to emancipate the mind. It allows us to fully use the precious resources of fine traditional Chinese culture in a broader cultural space and explore future-oriented theoretical and institutional innovations.

— Xi Jinping

Chapter I

The Rich Connotation and Vigorous Practice of "Second Integration"

Inside the compound of the Party School of the CPC Central Committee, there were three sets of statues: the one named "Comrades in Arms" is of Karl Marx and Friedrich Engels; the one named "Our Former Principal" is of Mao Zedong; and the third named "The Chief Architect" is of Deng Xiaoping. In March 2017, a new set of statutes joined them -- it is of ancient Chinese philosophers Confucius and Laozi.

Students of the Party School have a chance to visit Qufu, Shandong Province, where Confucius lived over two thousand years ago. They learn Confucian classics in the Confucian mansion and temple, researching and understanding the way of governance the ancient sage advocated. At the birthplace of Confucius, Nishan Forum has been held for many years, attended by researchers of Confucianism and Chinese culture worldwide.

China today witnesses the vibrant exchanges of ideas between the East and the West, between the past and the present, and between China and the outside world. Chinese modernization endows Chinese civilization with new strength, and Chinese civilization gives Chinese modernization a profound heritage. The practical exploration of the "Second Integration" theory keeps unfolding.

1. Upholding the Way: Organic Integration of Beliefs and Millennia-old Ideals

The "Second Integration" adapts communist and socialist beliefs to the millennial ideals of the Chinese nation, integrating the path of socialism with Chinese characteristics with the nation's traditions and civilizational heritage.

"When the path is just, the common good will reign over all under Heaven." This statement from the chapter of *Liyun, or The Conveyance of Rites,* in the Chinese classic *Liji, or The Book of Rites,* shows the way of governing the country and helping the world pursued by Chinese people with lofty ideals for thousands of years. Building a well-off society, achieving common prosperity, and realizing a world of great harmony have been the shared dream of noble-minded patriots in China through generations.

As a vanguard political party, the CPC has rallied people from all walks of life. From its humble beginning with about 50 founding members to more than 98 million today, the Party's growth over the past century owes much to integrating the basic tenets of Marxism with fine traditional Chinese culture. The millennial ideal of the Chinese has been transformed into the passionate belief and original aspiration of "seeking happiness of the Chinese people, striving for the rejuvenation of the Chinese nation, pursuing humanity's progress, and realizing global harmony."

A. Continuing to Strive for "the Happiness of the People"

In March 2023, Nangou Village, Yan'an, Shaanxi, experienced a spring rain, which prompted the large tract of orchards to enter the flowering period. A villager named Zhao Yongdong was busy working in a grove. His family's 20-mu orchard yielded him a net profit of over RMB 100,000 the year before. Modern agriculture and rural tourism have recently developed in this remote village on the Loess Plateau, lifting the villagers out of poverty. The village's per capita income has increased nearly four times in a decade.

After continuous efforts, China had won the largest poverty alleviation battle in human history, lifting 770 million impoverished rural people out of poverty by the end of 2021. China has thus eliminated its absolute poverty, creating a great miracle in the history of world poverty reduction. The 1.4 billion Chinese are living a well-off life, with an average life expectancy of more than 78 years and an annual per capita disposable income of RMB 35,000. The Chinese people's sense of fulfillment, happiness, and security is increasing day by day.

Standing at a new starting point and aiming at satisfying the "people's aspiration for a better life," China is writing a new chapter of seeking happiness for its people by improving the essential public service system and services, making development more balanced and its results more accessible to the people, and substantially promoting common prosperity.

B. Being Firm in the Belief of "Seeking Rejuvenation for the Nation"

Historians point out that ancient China once enjoyed a glorious era, with its economy consistently ranking first in the world. However, modern China fell behind in global modernization, experiencing a century of decline and humiliation after 1840. The country went through intense humiliation, the people were subjected to great pain and the Chinese civilization was plunged into darkness. At the critical moment of national peril, the CPC shouldered the historical responsibility of "seeking national rejuvenation" and fought for national independence and the people's liberation. It aimed to build a strong and prosperous nation and bring happiness to the people. The CPC has brought about profound changes in China through a century of struggle.

China has maintained its status as the world's second-largest economy for years. It also holds the top spot in terms of the scale of manufacturing. It has constructed the world's largest high-speed railway and expressway networks. The country has been accelerating its technological self-reliance and self-strengthening efforts, steadily advancing toward a nation of innovation.

C. Committed to the Ideal of Seeking Great Harmony for the World

The camel bells rang through the ancient Silk Road two thousand years ago, starting a journey of exchanges between Chinese and Western civilizations.

Today, the "steel camel caravan" roars westward: fully loaded China-Europe freight trains connect the East and the West again. In 2022 alone, 16,000 trains traversed Eurasia, transporting 1.6 million TEUs of goods.

In 2013, China launched the Belt and Road Initiative (BRI) to promote a human community with a shared future. In recent years, President Xi Jinping has put forward the Global Development Initiative, the Global Security Initiative, and the Global Civilization Initiative in the face of the rapidly evolving global landscape, which is undergoing significant changes not seen in a century. He emphasizes China's constructive role, highlighting its position as a builder of world peace, a contributor to global growth, a guardian of international order, and a promoter of human civilization progress.

Over the past decade, China has contributed an average of over 30% to global economic growth, becoming a vital engine for the recovery and development of the world economy and a prominent destination for transnational investments. Managing Director of the International Monetary Fund Kristalina Georgieva stated that China's economy is displaying positive momentum and will provide significant opportunities for other countries. From its independent and peaceful diplomacy to establishing a new type of international relations, China's series of actions on the world stage has played a "stabilizing" role in an otherwise turbulent world.

2. Advocating Etiquette: Organic Integration of Institutional Formation and Ritual-and-music Civilization

The "Second Integration" integrates the socialist system with Chinese characteristics with the ritual and music culture, endowing the modernization of China's system and capacity for governance with the strength of order, norms, and ethics.

"Etiquette keeps the universe in order," and "music harmonizes heaven and earth." In the Duke Wen of Zhou Temple in Qishan County, Shaanxi Province, sacrificial ceremonies were performed yearly to commemorate the duke for his ultimate virtue. The ritual and music system of the Western Zhou Dynasty, which originated three thousand years ago, represents a significant source of China's cosmology, worldview, societal perspective, and moral values that have been passed down through the ages. The tradition of the ritual and music culture resonates in a new fashion in modern China. The socialist system with Chinese characteristics, defined by upholding the CPC's leadership, constantly improves the modernization of China's system and capacity for governance.

A. Institutions Bring Effective Regulations

In the spring of 2023, the work on the application for UNESCO

World Cultural Heritage status for Beijing's Central Axis was in full swing. Cultural preservation organizations, working with enterprises, actively used advanced technology to develop the "Digital Central Axis," enabling better international dissemination and facilitating global understanding. The Central Axis of China's capital city holds unique cultural and symbolic significance. Here the millennial Chinese collective psyche of "grand unification," the philosophical thinking of "fulfilling centrality and harmony," and the tradition of orderly and balanced ceremonial protocols find contemporary expression.

Philosopher Lou Yulie said that when China was poor and weak a century ago, some Chinese thinkers sought to eliminate social evils and enlighten the Chinese. They claimed that the millennia-old ritual system was to blame. In fact, traditional Chinese rites and ethics have their merits. The essence of rituals and ethics is to help people understand their place in society and act according to established rules and norms. For example, respecting "Heaven, Earth, the State, Parents, and Teachers" is a virtue of traditional Chinese rites and ethics. Today, we should choose and apply these traditions wisely.

Sound political order is the key to modernizing "ritual order." From the perspective of governing the country, the rigorous self-governance of the Party since the 18th National Congress of the CPC has immense and far-reaching significance.

Adhering to and strengthening the centralized and unified leadership of the CPC Central Committee can be regarded as building a political order like the rules of a giant chess game with the Party sitting in the commanding post. Such a political order reflects the balance between order and vitality, stability and growth. It is the activation of the Chinese tradition of "ruling by etiquette" that emphasizes rules and order.

In 2019, the Fourth Plenary Session of the 19th Central Committee of the CPC reviewed and approved the "Decision on Some Major Issues Concerning How to Uphold and Improve the System of Socialism with Chinese Characteristics and Advance the Modernization of China's System and Capacity for Governance." It summarized 13 significant advantages of the socialist system with Chinese characteristics and the governance system, highlighted the adherence to and improvement of the fundamental, essential, and critical system, and vowed to build a systematic, scientific, standardized, and effective institutional system to better transform China's institutional advantages into governance effectiveness.

"The current system of political consultation, democratic decision-making, political supervision, and grassroots autonomy reflects not only the essence of Marxism but also the legacy of traditional Chinese culture," said Gao Guosheng, a scholar at the Central Institute of Socialism.

B. The Rule of Law Entails Strict Constraints

Facing the national flag, raising the right fist, and reciting the oath: "I pledge allegiance to the Constitution of the People's Republic of China ..." This scene has frequently appeared across the country since the implementation of the constitutional oath system in 2016. From national leaders to grassroots staff members, all employees of state organs must take the oath in public upon assuming office. The practice demonstrates China's firm determination to build a law-based government.

Honest and upright people have always been respected. The Duke of Shao of the Zhou Dynasty pioneered the inspection system around 1,000 BC. In the spring of 2023, over 30 family members of newly promoted senior officials lined up in the Duke of Shao Park in Baoji, Shaanxi Province, to champion the importance of family values and ethics.

Since the 18th National Congress of the CPC, the central leadership has demonstrated unprecedented courage and determination in boosting Party discipline and anti-corruption efforts. Over a decade, 553 officials registered at and supervised by the CPC

Central Committee have been investigated, and over 25,000 officials at the department and bureau level and more than 182,000 officials at the county and division level had been subjected to disciplinary measures. A clean and upright political environment within the CPC has continuously taken shape and developed. Through exploration, a successful path of relying on the Party's self-reform to break free from the historical rise-and-fall cycle of political power has formed.

C. Demonstration of Ethical Conduct and Cultivation of Able and Virtuous People

Society respects the virtuous and talented, families honor filial piety, and individuals emphasize self-improvement. The outstanding ethics and social norms in traditional Chinese culture are especially significant in today's world. Since the 18th National Congress of the CPC, the "new able and virtuous people in rural areas" system has emerged as an effective and complementary force in grassroots governance.

Wang Guoqiang, the Party chief of Gaocun Town in Shanxi Province, said the town has about 800 "new able and virtuous people in rural areas" out of a total population of 32,000. They serve as the "reserve force" for the village and township Party and administrative committees.

In Zhili Town, Zhejiang Province, a mediation team of the "new able and virtuous people in rural areas" was formed. Guided by the traditional Chinese concept of "mediation" and relying on family bonds, friendship, and deep affection for their native place, they have successfully mediated over 1,660 family disputes in eight years, gaining full recognition from the public.

3. Putting People First: Organic Integration of Development Philosophy and People-centered Doctrine

The "Second Integration" combines people-centered development thought with people-oriented thinking that has prevailed in China for five thousand years, endowing the governance concept with a deep sense of the people.

"The people are the foundation of a country, and only when the people lead a good life, can the country thrive." The people-oriented thinking is an essential component of traditional Chinese political culture, reflecting the governing philosophy of ancient China.

The CPC adheres to the Marxist view of historical materialism and further develops the fundamental tenet that "the people are the creators of history." This fundamental principle, integrated with Chinese realities, treats the traditional concept of people-oriented thinking discerningly. The CPC selectively inherits and creatively draws upon the reasonable core of simple, people-centered ideas. The Party has put forward a people-centered philosophy of development and enriched and developed the theoretical system of socialism with Chinese characteristics, realizing the historical transcendence of the people-oriented thinking from the perspective of political standpoint and value orientation.

A. Development for the People

The CPC has its foundation in the people. So does its strength. The CPC has put people at the center of all its endeavors since its founding. People-centeredness remains the most distinctive feature of the CPC.

"Chinese people's well-being is a national priority." "Our mission is to meet the Chinese people's aspiration for a better life." "This country is its people; the people are the country. As the CPC has led the Chinese people in fighting to establish and develop the People's Republic, it has really been fighting for their support...." Xi Jinping made those remarks on different occasions.

"Bear in mind what concerns the people and act upon what they hope for." As members of the governing party, CPC officials uphold and implement those principles in their practical work.

B. Development by Relying on the People

"Water can carry a boat and may also overturn it." The traditional Chinese people-oriented thinking puts "people" in such a critical position that it relates to a country's survival. Drawing on the essential idea of "emphasizing the people," the CPC underscores the respect for the principal position of the people and relies on the people to achieve rapid economic development and long-term social stability.

The Chinese people have always been the "main force" in the fight against poverty and pandemics and in the undertakings to promote reform, control contamination, and fend off risks.

The Chinese people directly participate in system design, legislation, and policy-making, becoming the masters of the country in its true sense. In August 2020 alone, netizens made over a million comments concerning the preparation of the 14th Five-year Plan. More than a thousand of the suggestions were adopted.

Lintao County in Gansu Province set up one of the country's first local outreach offices for national legislation. It has participated in the solicitation of opinions on 70 draft laws. For example, township official Yang Xin's suggestion was incorporated into *Rural Revitalization Promotion Law*. "Grassroots officials can also directly participate in national legislation. Democracy must be as visible and tangible as such," Yang said.

C. Results of Development to be Enjoyed by the People

Robert Lawrence Kuhn, chairman of the American Kuhn Foundation, has kept track of China's development for over 30 years. He believes that the "people-centered" development philosophy is the cornerstone of the CPC's policies. Efforts to promote poverty alleviation and common prosperity are strong evidence of the philosophy.

China has effectively solved the problem of providing adequate food and clothing for its 1.4 billion people. In the past decade, nearly 100 million rural poor residents were lifted out of poverty, over 400 million people joined the middle-income group, and per capita disposable income for residents doubled. China has also built the world's most extensive education, social security, and healthcare systems. The vision of ensuring that every child receives nurturing care, everyone has access to education, everyone earns a decent income, everyone receives medical treatment when they are ill, everyone is well taken care of in their old age, everyone has a place to live, and every vulnerable group receives necessary support has gradually become a reality.

4. Respecting Morality: Organic Integration of Core Values and Traditional Moral Orientation

The "Second Integration" integrates core socialist values with the traditional Chinese value orientation.

The ideas of "constantly striving to become stronger" and "promoting growth with great virtue" have their roots in the ancient Chinese classic, the *Book of Changes* (*I Ching*). These and numerous other philosophical ideas in various classics have shaped the tradition of respecting morality that has lasted for over 2,000 years in Chinese culture and is now integrated into China's governing philosophy. Fine traditional Chinese culture always embraces a profound pursuit of moral integrity.

A nation cannot thrive without strong spiritual strength. The Chinese ethos are the soul of national rejuvenation and strength, encompassing not only the essence of traditional Chinese virtues but also core socialist values. They form ever-growing and enduring spiritual strength that has been passed down from generation to generation. Upholding the national spirit centered on patriotism and the spirit of our times centered on reform and innovation has become a powerful driving force for advancing socialism with Chinese characteristics.

A. With the Core Values as the Guiding Principle

How to forge the Chinese ethos in the new era? In November 2012, the report to the 18th National Congress of the CPC formally proposed a set of core socialist values. The highly condensed "24 characters" are divided into three levels: Prosperity, democracy, civility, and harmony are the value requirements at the national level. Freedom, equality, justice, and the rule of law are the value requirements at the societal level. Patriotism, dedication, integrity, and friendliness are the value requirements at the individual level.

"This generalization actually answers the major questions of what kind of country we want to build, what kind of society we want to build, and what kind of citizens we want to cultivate,"[1] said Xi Jinping in May 2014.

From establishing exemplary families and campuses to forming centers for promoting cultural and ethical advancement in urban and rural areas, core socialist values have been widely integrated into all aspects of social life.

The bulletin board of a community center for promoting cultural and ethical advancement in Jiayuguan City, Gansu Province, displays the governance innovations of the local government. They borrowed from the ancient classic *Guanzi* the governance thought of "taking the family as the family, the township as the township, the country as the

---

[1] Xi Jinping, "Youth Should Consciously Practice the Core Socialist Values," On the CPC's Work on Youth, CPC Central Party Literature Press, 2022, p72.

country, and the world as the world." They proposed the working idea of "Good Governance in the Impregnable Pass (a historical reference to the city) with Five Ways of Governance Well Integrated," emphasizing the role of political guidance, the rule of law, moral and ethical standards, self-governance, and enhanced governance capacity.

B. The Key is Officials' Political Morality

The demonstrative examples of pioneer models are vital to carrying forward the core socialist values to implement the national spirit and the spirit of the times. CPC officials are the backbone of society. Therefore, it is essential to do an excellent job morally cultivating these few key officials. Xi Jinping repeatedly emphasized that CPC members "should be committed to the greater good, uphold public morality and keep personal integrity."

To be committed to the greater good is to love the Party and country, to uphold public morality is to maintain good social manners, and to keep personal integrity is to cultivate oneself.

Jining City in Shandong Province uses fine traditional Chinese culture to enhance the cultivation of Party officials' political morality and has put a lot of thought into building an education base aiming at boosting officials' political morality: the Officials' Political Morality Education College. The base develops on-site experiential teaching courses at the Confucian Mansion and Temple in Qufu and the Mencius Temple in Zoucheng, allowing students to experience the values of fine traditional culture in line with the times and enhance their cultural self-confidence. The Organization Department of the CPC Central Committee has arranged for over 1,300 middle-aged and young students to come to the base in 12 batches to receive political and moral education. After the training, many students returned to Jining with their children or colleagues to further share insights on traditional culture.

C. The Rule of Virtue and the Rule of Law Complement Each Other

Law is written morality, which is the law of a person's inner world. China insists on combining law-based governance with the governance by virtue, emphasizing the regulatory and educative roles of ethics. It aims to achieve a complementary relationship between law and ethics with law-based governance and the governance by virtue reinforcing each other.

By combining autonomy, law-based governance and governance by virtue, China has established a new pattern of grassroots management in urban and rural areas. There are 492,000 village committees and 116,000 residents' committees nationwide, which are elected by the residents. In the new round of grassroots autonomous organization elections completed in 2021, hundreds of millions voted to elect nearly 2.8 million villagers' (residents') committee members.

5. Perspective of the Intrinsic Laws of Cultural Inheritance and Development

The "Second Integration" endows the national rejuvenation with cultural roots and spirit by adapting socialist advanced culture to fine traditional Chinese culture.

"By contemplating the forms existing in the Heaven, we understand the time and its changing demands. Through contemplation of the forms existing in human society, we find it possible to shape the world." Traditional Chinese cultural beliefs originate from this sentence from the *Book of Changes*. The Marxist view of culture holds that culture stems from people's social practice of understanding and transforming nature while reacting to practice. It is inherently connected with the Chinese thought of "the ornamental observances of society being able to transform all under heaven."

In today's Chinese political narrative, culture is divided into three parts: fine traditional Chinese culture, revolutionary culture, and advanced socialist culture. These three cultures may have formed in different ways and at different times. But they are inseparable, eventually merging into a socialist culture with Chinese characteristics.

To develop socialist culture with Chinese characteristics means to create a socialist culture for our nation — a culture that is sound and people-oriented; that embraces modernization, the world, and the future; and that both promotes material and socialist cultural-ethical advancement. In developing this culture, we must follow the guidance of Marxism, base our efforts on Chinese culture, and consider the realities of contemporary China and the conditions of the present era."[1] The root and soul of national rejuvenation lie in fine traditional Chinese culture."

A. To Cultivate People with Culture: Immersing People's Minds in Classics

Tourists from all over the country visit San Su Shrine in Meishan City, Sichuan Province, all year round. They make a memorable trip to pay respect to the models of ancient Chinese literati: Su Xun, Su Shi, and Su Zhe from the same family. The Chinese have recited their poems and prose for hundreds of years.

---

[1] Xi Jinping, "Secure a Decisive Victory in Building a Moderately Prosperous Society in All Respects and Strive for the Great Success of Socialism with Chinese Characteristics for a New Era," Xi Jinping on the Governance of China, III, Foreign Languages Press, 2020, p.32.

Xi Jinping visited this place on June 8, 2022. He said, "A drop of water can reflect the sun, and the San Su Shrine can demonstrate the profoundness of our Chinese culture. When we say we must firm up our cultural confidence, we have the three Su's in China, an important example of fine traditional Chinese culture."[1]

Culture provides norms, ways, and environments for communal living. In the 5,000 years of Chinese civilization, culture has played an essential role in educating people, cultivating them, and unifying their minds. Splendid cultural activities are witnessed nationwide, centering around the mission of "upholding socialism with Chinese characteristics, rallying public support, fostering a new generation of young people, developing Chinese culture, and better presenting China to the world."

B. Utilizing Cultural Artifacts to Bring History to Life

The street lights come on along the Qujiang River in Xi'an City. The magnificent scenery of the Tang Dynasty and the modern spectacle complement each other in brilliance. In the immersive experience of Tang culture, the tourists dressed in Tang and Han costumes find

---

[1] "On his Inspection Tour of San Su Shrine, the General Secretary Mentioned Three Key Words," Xinhua News Agency, June 11, 2022.

it hard to tear themselves away from the city's enchanting tourist attractions.

The Shaanxi Culture Industry Investment Group, the operator of the Longest Day in Chang'an program, has been committed to "searching for contemporary values in history and exploring the modern expression of traditional culture." Wang Yong, the group's board chairman, said that fine traditional Chinese culture is a precious resource in integrating culture with tourism. With tourism adding extra charm to culture, culture remains the soul of tourism. As a result, history and culture are both "appealing" and "profitable."

It has become a new trend in Chinese cultural heritage utilization to bring to life the cultural relics collected in museums, the cultural heritage displayed on the vast land, and the texts written in ancient books. In recent years, the "archeology craze," the "museum craze," and the "intangible cultural heritage craze" have become extremely popular, and creative cultural production has boomed beyond expectation. The inheritance of culture and the continuation of civilization enrich people's lives with intangible nourishment and power through popular activities and events suiting all tastes.

C. To Cultivate and Transform Society with Culture

Culture guides social tendencies. In recent years, all parts of

China have vigorously implemented projects to inherit and develop fine traditional Chinese culture, improve public cultural service systems, create cities with high-level of civility, and revitalize villages, advocating the central theme of social norms to boost positive energy. As a result, people live and work in peace and contentment, society is stable and orderly, and the levels of social civility have been elevated.

The integration of advanced socialist culture with fine traditional Chinese culture has enhanced social civility, promoted openness and inclusiveness, and boosted innovation and creation.

"Vehicles giving the right of way to pedestrians" leads to social harmony, waste sorting makes the best use of everything, "new citizens" (unregistered urban residents) enjoy equal education and healthcare resources, citizens' affairs are handled online, and farmers use intelligent technology ... New customs and styles have heralded a new chapter of a better life in contemporary China's urban and rural areas.

6. Valuing Harmony: Organic Integration of the Concept of a Human Community with a Shared Future and the Path of Harmonious Coexistence Among Nations

The "Second Integration" combines the concept of a human community with a shared future with foreign relations between all nations in harmony and endows the new form of human civilization with a thorough mutual understanding of ideas.

Traditionally, the Chinese embraced the ideas of "being truthful and harmonious with their neighbors," "being benevolent and friendly to them," "valuing harmony above all," and "harmoniously coexisting among various nations." Ten years ago, Xi Jinping put forward "building a human community with a shared future," integrating ancient wisdom into the new concept.

In today's world, the trend of peace, development, cooperation, and win-win endeavors is unstoppable. However, growing deficits in global peace, development, security, and governance pose unprecedented challenges to human society. China has always adhered to the diplomatic principles of upholding peace and promoting common development and is committed to fostering a human community with a shared future. Within the diverse forms of human civilization, China's ideas shine brightly.

A. Harmony in Diversity: Respecting the Diversified World Civilizations

"Harmony in diversity" is an ancient Chinese philosophy passed down for over two thousand years. The Nestorian Stele, collected by the Forest of Stone Steles Museum in Xi'an, Shaanxi Province, China, records the historical facts of Roman missionaries preaching in China during the Tang Dynasty, reflecting China's respect for foreign cultures.

Quanzhou City in Fujian Province has long been known as a place where "seven religions converge." Houses of worship of Buddhism, Daoism, Christianity, Catholicism, Muslim, and Hinduism coexist harmoniously even to this day.

Civilizations may be different, but they are never superior or inferior to one another. In March 2023, Xi Jinping proposed the Global Civilization Initiative to promote inclusive coexistence and mutual learning among different civilizations and contribute Chinese wisdom to this endeavor. The initiative advocates for a civilization perspective based on equality, mutual understanding, dialogue, and inclusiveness. It encourages cultural exchanges that transcend estrangement, mutual learning that goes beyond clashes, and coexistence that surpasses feelings of superiority.

B. Common Goals: Promoting Shared Values for All Humanity

China proposed a set of common values for humanity — peace, development, fairness, justice, democracy, and freedom. These values not only originate from Marxist ideology but also incorporate elements of fine traditional Chinese culture.

In promoting peace, China has established an 8,000-strong standby peacekeeping force and has dispatched over 50,000 peacekeeping personnel to nearly 30 UN peacekeeping missions. China has also established the China-UN Peace and Development Fund, becoming the second-largest contributor and an essential troop-contributing country to UN peacekeeping operations. Over the years, China has actively engaged in mediation and negotiation efforts in various regional hot spots.

In promoting development, China has proposed the establishment of the Asian Infrastructure Investment Bank (AIIB) and supported the establishment of the New Development Bank (NDB). China has also facilitated the reform of the International Monetary Fund (IMF) quota system and participated in formulating governance rules in emerging areas. China has made significant efforts to help developing countries find paths to prosperity, actively sharing its own experiences in poverty alleviation. China has repeatedly announced unconditional exemptions for heavily indebted poor and least developed countries from their interest-free government loans due to China.

In upholding fairness and justice, China does not follow the Western path of colonial plunder or tread the crooked path of seeking hegemony when becoming strong. China firmly opposes hegemonism and power politics, advocating equality among countries regardless of their size, strength, or wealth. China supports unity and a win-win mindset to address complex global challenges, aiming to create a just and equitable international environment.

C. Great Harmony Under Heaven: Building a Human Community with a Shared Future

Lichun, or the Beginning of the Spring, is the first of the 24 solar terms in the traditional Chinese lunar calendar. In 2022, it fell on February 4. On this day, a spectacular opening ceremony was held for the Beijing Winter Olympics, catching the world's attention. Snowflakes gathered together, igniting the torch that symbolizes peace. Against the backdrop of the COVID-19 pandemic, the scene was particularly thought-provoking, reminding people that humanity is a united family with a shared future.

By promoting the building of a community with a shared future for humanity, China does not seek to replace one system with another or one civilization with another. Instead, it aims to find common ground for building a better world among various nations. This concept not only draws inspiration from the essence of the traditional Chinese idea of *"tianxia"* (all under Heaven) and the culture of harmony but also represents a creative development of the Marxist concept of "community."

The Belt and Road Initiative is a significant practical platform for promoting the construction of a human community with a shared future. According to a World Bank report, the joint efforts in implementing the Belt and Road Initiative will help lift 7.6 million people out of extreme poverty and 32 million out of moderate poverty in the participating countries.

Diseases are the common enemy of all humanity. Over the past 60 years, China has dispatched 30,000 medical workers to 76 countries and regions in Africa, Asia, the Americas, Europe, and Oceania, providing medical assistance to a total of 290 million patients.

Climate change is a common challenge faced by humankind. China has carried out climate dialogue and practical cooperation with countries worldwide and has achieved remarkable results, making historic and vital contributions to the conclusion, signing, entry into force, and implementation of the Paris Agreement. China has signed memorandums of understanding on South-South cooperation on climate change with dozens of developing countries.

It is natural to integrate the basic tenets of Marxism with China's specific realities and fine traditional culture if we are to create and develop socialism with Chinese characteristics based on the profound Chinese civilization of more than 5,000 years. This is the understanding we have drawn from our exploration of the path of socialism with Chinese characteristics and the key to our success.

— Xi Jinping

Chapter II

Historical Roots and Innovation of the "Second Integration"

The CPC has been able to overcome various tests and hardships over the past century because it has been constantly adapting Marxism to the Chinese context and has been committed to theoretical innovation and creation.

The report to the 20th National Congress of the CPC pointed out that "only by integrating the basic tenets of Marxism with China's specific realities and fine traditional culture and only by applying dialectical and historical materialism can we provide correct answers to the major questions presented by the times and discovered through practice and can we ensure that Marxism always retains its vigor and vitality."

"It is necessary to summarize previous theories to initiate new ideas." The "Two Integrations" proposed by Xi Jinping, especially the "Second Integration," are not only an all-encompassing summary of history and a profound revelation of laws but also a correct guidance for theoretical innovation and development. They demonstrate a high level of the sense of history and cultural confidence, achieving a new leap forward and opening up a new realm for adapting Marxism to the Chinese context and the needs of the times.

1. Identifying the Point of Convergence: Penetrating the Social Fabric Unconsciously

The prerequisite for "integration" is mutual compatibility. Marxism and fine traditional Chinese culture have different origins but exhibit a high degree of compatibility. Only through mutual compatibility can they organically integrate with each other. After Marxism was introduced into China, the idea of scientific socialism was warmly welcomed by the Chinese people and finally took root in the soil of China to blossom and bear fruit. That is not accidental. It is because of the integration of Marxism with China's excellent history and culture passed down for thousands of years and with the values that the majority of the Chinese embrace in daily life.

A. A High Degree of Alignment in Value Propositions

Marxism envisions an ideal society of communism. Meanwhile, fine traditional Chinese culture regards the ideal of "common good that reigns over all under Heaven when justice prevails" as the highest political pursuit and the people-oriented thought based on the concept of "people being a nation's foundation, which stabilizes the nation" as the fundamental political belief. It also takes the idea of "cultivating moral characters, putting one's own houses in order, running the country well, and letting peace prevail on earth" as the logic for practice. Fine traditional Chinese culture permeates the political ethics of "identifying the family with the same structure of the country" characterized by the assumption that "the whole world is one family." Both Marxism and fine traditional Chinese culture hope to build a beautiful society free from oppression and exploitation, where everyone is equal and free.

In his speech at the ceremony commemorating the bicentenary of the birth of Karl Marx on May 4, 2018, Xi Jinping emphasized nine aspects of studying Marx. These nine aspects demonstrate the convergence between the basic tenets of Marxism and fine traditional Chinese culture where values are concerned. For example, Marxist thought on the patterns underlying the development of human society, namely, human society would ultimately move toward communism as an inevitable trend, corresponds to the idea of "Great Harmony" embraced by ancient Chinese. Marxism's perspective on the relationship between man and nature resonates with China's philosophy -- "the harmony between heaven and humanity." Marxism's ideas about world history happen to align with the traditional Chinese concept of "*tianxia*" (all under Heaven). As a result, Marxism and fine traditional Chinese culture have become the primary sources contributing to the concept of "a human community with a shared future."

The report to the 20th National Congress of the CPC further clarifies the alignment of these two at the level of values. It points out that some aspects of the Chinese people's worldview, perspective on the world, social outlook, and moral values accumulated through long-term production and daily life are highly compatible with the advocated values of scientific socialism. It makes the phenomenon of "intuitively applying them in daily life" an essential characteristic of the "Second Integration."

As Marxism of contemporary China and of the 21st century, Xi Jinping Thought on Socialism with Chinese Characteristics for a New Era resonates with fine traditional Chinese culture at the level of values. Therefore, it can go deep into the hearts of the Chinese people and integrate into the Chinese cultural genes.

B. A High Degree of Alignment Between the View of Practice and Practical Rationality

Philosopher Tang Yijie once stated that both Marxism and Confucianism emphasize practice. Marxism's most important theoretical qualities lie in upholding the principle of starting from reality, integrating theory with practice, seeking truth from facts, and testing and developing truth through practice. Moreover, traditional Chinese culture also has a fine tradition of materialism. Many insightful materialistic viewpoints have been proposed by the ancient philosophers such as Guanzi and Mencius of the pre-Qin eras to such scholars as Wang Fuzhi, Yan Yuan, Dai Zhen, and Wei Yuan of the Qing Dynasty. The practical rationality embedded in traditional Chinese culture is also an essential cultural and psychological base that facilitates the acceptance of Marxism by the Chinese people.

Traditional Chinese culture is not exclusive. On the contrary, it cherishes the idea of "thriving by embracing each other like the sea welcoming all rivers." In a word, it is good at absorbing all the outstanding achievements of human civilizations. The victory of the October Revolution in Russia enabled modern Chinese intellectuals to experience the practical power of Marxism-Leninism in transforming the old world more directly. As a result, they turned to studying and disseminating Marxism-Leninism one after another. The early intellectuals who were the first to accept Marxism-Leninism integrated the practical character of Marxism with the historical wisdom of fine traditional Chinese culture that advocates studying ancient classics to meet present needs. At the most critical moments of modern China, the power of Marxist truth revitalized the great civilization that the Chinese nation had created over thousands of years.

2. Keeping the Root and Spirit Alive: Steadily Charting a New Course Amid Changing Times

"Only a river with a far-reaching source can flow longer, and only trees with deep roots can grow with thick foliage." The "Second Integration" regards culture as the "root and spirit," adapts to the times, and profoundly integrates the power of culture into the nation's vitality, creativity, and cohesion. The "integration" has solidified the foundation of the path, enabling socialism with Chinese characteristics to have a broader and deeper historical depth and expanding the cultural foundation of socialism with Chinese characteristics. Modernization through a Chinese path empowers Chinese civilization with modern strength, while Chinese civilization endows modernization through a Chinese path with a profound heritage.

A. The Historical Choice of Preserving Cultural Heritage and Continuity

The CPC is not only an active leader and practitioner of advanced Chinese culture but also a faithful inheritor and promoter of fine traditional Chinese culture. As early as the New Democratic Revolution, Mao Zedong, one of the first-generation CPC leaders, pointed out, "Studying our historical heritage and critically summarizing it with the methods of Marxism is another task of our learning."

Fine traditional Chinese culture is the spiritual heritage of China and its nation. It needs to be inherited from generation to generation and advanced with the times with the ability to weed through the old to bring forth the new. Xi Jinping incisively pointed out, "Fine traditional Chinese culture is the crystallization of the wisdom and the essence of Chinese civilization. It is the root and soul of the Chinese nation, providing us with a solid foundation to stand firm amidst the tide of world cultures."[1]

Since the 18th National Congress of the CPC, the CPC Central

---

[1] Xinhua News Agency, "Xi Jinping presided over the 39th group study session of the Political Bureau of the CPC Central Committee and delivered an important speech," May 28, 2022.

Committee with Comrade Xi Jinping at the core has been steadfastly adhering to dialectical materialism and historical materialism. With an objective, scientific, and respectful attitude, it has been committed to discarding what needs to be discarded, transforming what needs to be transformed, and innovating what needs to be innovated, striving to make the most basic cultural genes of the Chinese nation adapt to contemporary culture and coordinate with modern society. The CPC sticks to integrating the idea of "strengthening the foundation and nurturing the roots" with the notion of "upholding the tradition while fostering innovation" to conduct in-depth research into new situations and emerging issues under the new conditions of the new era. While inheriting fine traditional Chinese culture, the CPC has also accomplished creative transformation and innovative development, ensuring that the strength of the Chinese culture is continuously inherited and revitalized.

B. The Scientific Choice for Promoting the Great Rejuvenation

Today's China is standing majestically in the east of the world, and it is closer to, more confident about, and capable of realizing national rejuvenation than at any time in history. Fine traditional Chinese culture contains the endless inner strength of the Chinese nation, records its long-standing cultural memory, and is the civilizational foundation for realizing China's national rejuvenation.

The Chinese nation cannot rejuvenate without solid cultural confidence and prosperity. Cultural confidence is a broader, deeper, and more fundamental form of confidence. The "unique cultural tradition" is the "primary reason" for choosing the path of socialism with Chinese characteristics. Xi Jinping traced the roots of socialism with Chinese characteristics to the "inheritance and development of Chinese civilization of over five thousand years," using culture to connect China's history of civilization development. He emphasized that the national governance system results from long-term development, progressive improvement, and endogenous evolution based on China's historical inheritance, cultural traditions, and socioeconomic development. His statement fully demonstrates that China's confidence in the chosen path, theory and system all boil down to cultural confidence built upon a foundation of over five thousand years of civilization.

Building upon cultural confidence, the report to the 20th National Congress of the CPC for the first time put forward the concept of "cultural confidence and strength," further highlighting the importance of culture as the "root and soul" of the Chinese nation on the path to advance the great rejuvenation of the Chinese nation.

C. The Inevitable Choice amidst the Impact of Diverse Ideological Currents

Currently, ideas and culture impact each other worldwide, leading to significant changes in social ideology. Since the beginning of reform and opening up, China has absorbed excellent elements of world culture and civilization humbly on the one hand. On the other hand, erroneous trends such as money-worship, hedonism, and egocentricity have occasionally occurred. Historical and cultural nihilism has appeared in the Chinese intellectual sphere. Some equate modernization with Westernization and uphold the so-called "universal values" representing Western values as the criterion, which has seriously affected people's thinking and the social discourse environment.

Facing the onslaught of various foreign trends of thought and detrimental endogenous thinking, Xi Jinping emphasizes the importance of "becoming prouder, more confident, and more assured in the identity of Chinese people." He repeatedly pointed out that it is necessary to understand the source of strength of the Chinese nation from fine traditional Chinese culture. He said, "Fine traditional Chinese culture has become the genetic heritage of the Chinese nation, deeply rooted in the hearts of the Chinese people, and subtly influenced their ways of thinking and behavior. Today, as we advocate a set of core socialist values, we must draw abundant nourishment from it; otherwise, it will lack vitality and influence."[1]

In the context of the social transformation in the new era, fine traditional culture plays a crucial role in neutralizing the impact of diverse cultural values and in cultivating core socialist values. It is thus imperative to inherit and promote it vigorously.

3. Restoring Vitality: Building Bridges through "Two Inclusions" and "Two Innovations"

Critical inheritance is the methodology of Marxism. Guided by the Marxist worldview and methodology, Xi Jinping has inherited and developed the scientific approach adopted by the CPC toward traditional culture, insisting on applying the past to the present, drawing lessons from history, and treating tradition with discernment while discarding what is outdated. Neither giving an excessive emphasis on the past at the expanse of the present nor rejecting the past as irrelevant to the present, he stresses achieving creative transformation and innovative development of traditional culture and integrating the

---

[1] Xinhua News Agency, "Speech by Xi Jinping at a Symposium with Teachers and Students of Peking University," May 4, 2014.

essence of Marxist ideology with the refined essence of fine traditional Chinese culture and with the shared values embraced by the Chinese people.

A. Identifying the Root Problems: Valuing Tradition without Advocating for a Return to the Past

Cultural nihilism completely denies traditional culture, while cultural conservatism unconditionally affirms traditional culture. They use the concept of "time-honored tradition" to oppose modernization and the idea of "enduring orthodoxy" to resist adapting Marxism to the Chinese context. They simplistically interpret the great rejuvenation of the Chinese nation as the revival of traditional culture. Some negative ideological trends have emerged under the guise of "traditional culture."

Culture possesses distinct historical characteristics and is the product of the practical human activities. In its formation and development, traditional culture inevitably reflects the limitations and influences of people's cognitive level, historical conditions, and social systems of that time. Consequently, it may contain outdated elements or aspects that have become obsolete. When it comes to traditional Chinese culture, it should not be mindlessly and uncritically copied. It can be considered outstanding only by eliminating the dross and preserving the essence.

Once grasped by the majority, advanced cultural ideas can be transformed into a powerful material force. Conversely, if backward or erroneous notions are not overcome, they can impede social development and progress. Since its establishment, the CPC has always attached importance to distinguishing the essence from the dross in traditional culture. Xi Jinping, from the perspective of historical materialism, affirmed the characteristics and advantages of traditional culture while dialectically pointing out its shortcomings and inadequacies. He emphasized guiding CPC members, especially leading officials, to resist and oppose decadent political cultures, such as the misuse of *guanxi* (personal connections and networks), the art of cunning and deceit, bureaucratic maneuvering, and unwritten rules. He also underscored leading the entire society in actively cultivating and practicing core socialist values, establishing a sound moral atmosphere, and preventing the resurgence of feudal and decadent ethical culture.

B. Cultivating a Righteous Mind and Pursuing the Right Path to Activate Traditional Culture with Marxism

The Confucian theory about the relationship between knowledge and practice runs through traditional Chinese culture. The essence of such a relationship is embodied by the idea that when one possesses the supreme virtue of a sage within oneself and applies it to the external world, one would become a true king where governance is concerned. Since the rise of neo-Confucianism in the Song and Ming dynasties, traditional Chinese culture had increasingly become rigid and conservative. From the "knowledge-action" perspective, Confucian scholars emphasized "inner sagehood," which refers to cultivating inner virtues and character. However, they often overlooked the importance of "outer kinghood," which involves the practical application of those virtues in the external world. Consequently, they found themselves trapped in a dilemma of "idly discussing inner virtues, only to be willing to sacrifice their lives for the ruler in times of crisis," leaving them powerless and unable to respond effectively to changes and challenges.

Through his brilliant work "On Practice," Mao Zedong revitalized the traditional concept of knowledge and action by proposing "applying the Marxist theory to practice." On this basis, Xi Jinping further developed the idea of knowledge and action. He emphasized the unity of knowledge and action, promoting action through knowledge and emphasizing practical work. He sharply criticized the "double-faced" behavior of "acting one way in someone's presence and another behind his back, or speaking one way while acting another"—a behavior marked by knowing without acting or knowing one thing but acting another way.

"A challenge Xi Jinping faces is to prevent China from becoming a country without an independent culture and spirit. He has to awaken and modernize China's outstanding traditional cultural genes," commented a foreign scholar.[1]

In the face of unprecedented global changes, how can we grasp the profound value of fine traditional Chinese culture by adapting to the changes in the world and the era? The answer lies in the "Second Integration."

"The basic tenets of Marxism combine with fine traditional Chinese culture," in which the word "combine" highlights the dominant position of Marxism in the "Second Integration." Activating fine traditional Chinese culture with Marxist positions, viewpoints, and methods in an objective, scientific, and respectful attitude can better integrate Marxism with contemporary Chinese practice and align it with the theme of the era of national rejuvenation.

Chinese Communists have developed a correct understanding of the dialectical unity and resonance between Marxism and fine

---

[1] James C. Hsiung (US), "Traditional Culture Is a Unique Strategic Resource," Study Times, http://theory.people.com.cn/GB/n1/2016/0617/c376186-28453910.html

traditional Chinese culture. Per the requirements of dialectical materialism and historical materialism, through the "Second Integration," they have conducted a scientific assessment and made correct selections regarding traditional Chinese culture. Only through this process can the Chinese nation's most fundamental cultural genes be activated, enabling them to adapt to contemporary culture and coordinate with modern society.

C. Contributing to Social Stability and Order by Adhering to Proper Rites and Norms: Creative Transformation and Innovative Development

How can the integration of the basic tenets of Marxism with fine traditional Chinese culture be achieved? The key lies in creative transformation and innovative development. Take the term "original aspiration" as an example. It first appeared in *"Soushenji"* (*In Search of the Supernatural*) from the Jin Dynasty, meaning the original wish or belief.

In the report to the 19th National Congress of the CPC, Xi Jinping emphasized, "The original aspiration and the mission of Chinese Communists is to seek happiness for the Chinese people and rejuvenation for the Chinese nation." The long-lost term "original aspiration" has been reactivated by being given a new meaning by integrating the Marxist Party spirit with the traditional culture of self-cultivation to inspire the Chinese Communists to keep devoting themselves to the new era. "Original aspiration" became a household buzzword in China in 2017.

The promotion of traditional culture has happened not only in politics. Over the past decade, "creative transformation and innovative development" in the cultural sector have deeply penetrated Chinese people's lives.

Classical dances like the "Night Banquet in the Tang Palace" and the "Journey of a Legendary Landscape Painting" became a hit as soon as they debuted. TV programs such as "Chinese Poetry Conference" and "China in Classics" triggered a craze for reading poetry and studying classics. The new archaeological discoveries in historical sites like Sanxingdui and Liangzhu have ignited the public's enthusiasm for cultural relics. On April 18, 2023, the Dunhuang Academy in Gansu Province, in collaboration with Tencent, launched an online platform of "Digital Cave of Buddhist Scriptures." Modern high technology has revitalized the millennium-old historical site, instantly allowing the world to appreciate Chinese stories and aesthetics.

Through the "Second Integration," fine traditional Chinese culture undergoes creative evolution and development. The ideological concepts, humanistic spirit, and moral standards therein are fully explored, giving rise to new connotations that transcend time and possess contemporary value. With the integration of artistic creativity and Chinese cultural values, as well as the fusion of Chinese aesthetics and contemporary aesthetic pursuits, the spirit of the times revitalized the vitality of fine traditional Chinese culture, making it welcome among the public. It ultimately promoted the integration of the essence of Marxist ideology with the essence of fine traditional Chinese culture and the common values that people intuitively apply in their everyday lives.

4. Facilitating New Leaps Forward: Exploring Innovative Theories in Step with the Times

Continuously writing a new chapter of adapting Marxism to the Chinese context and the needs of our times is the solemn responsibility of contemporary Chinese Communists. The "Second Integration" continuously consolidates the historical and popular foundations for adapting Marxism to the Chinese context and the needs of our times, firmly rooting Marxism in China. Meanwhile, the "Second Integration" represents another liberation of thinking, enabling China to fully use the precious resources of fine traditional Chinese culture within a broader cultural space, exploring theoretical and institutional innovations for the future.

A. Transformation Power: Promoting the Popularization of Marxism

Since the introduction of Marxism to China, how to deal with the relationship between Marxism and traditional Chinese culture has become a major theoretical and practical issue. The Chinese Communists gave a scientific answer: Chinese Marxists are, first and foremost, "Chinese". Marxist theory is not a dogma but an action guide and must develop with changes in practice. The history of the development of Marxism is the history of its continued development at the hands of Marx, Engels, and their successors in accordance with developments in time, practice, and knowledge. This history is one of continued self-refinement by absorbing all human history's redoubtable cultural and intellectual achievements. Over the past 100 years, Marxism has profoundly changed China, and China has also greatly enriched Marxism.

The "First Integration" achieved the initial leap forward in adapting Marxism to the Chinese context. The contemporary Chinese Communists, with Comrade Xi Jinping as their chief representative, have deepened their understanding of the laws governing the adaption of Marxism to the Chinese context and modernization of Marxism through the "Second Integration" with a high level of historical consciousness and unwavering cultural confidence. They take Chinese civilization as the source of living water and inherit the essence of humanistic spirit, moral values, and historical wisdom from the splendid civilization of more than 5,000 years. By integrating the ideological essence of Marxism with the spiritual characteristics of fine traditional Chinese culture, they have been fortifying the historical heritage and cultural foundation of socialism with Chinese characteristics.

The "Second Integration" opens a new chapter of modernizing and localizing Marxism in China. By grounding itself in the reality of China and responding to the needs of the times, it takes confident strides forward in the direction guided by "Chinese wisdom."

B. Centripetal Force: Continuing to Promote the Process from Popularization to "Intuitive Daily Application"

The philosophical concepts, moral ideals, values, and practical wisdom in fine traditional Chinese culture have enriched and enhanced Marxism. By promoting the integration of the basic tenets of Marxism with the values and modes of thinking found in fine traditional Chinese culture, Marxism was transformed from being "in China" to "being shaped by China." As Mao Zedong pointed out, "'Adaptation to the Chinese context' means thorough and comprehensive transformation from within and without," gradually making the process a reality.

Because of this, Marxism has a stronger historical and cultural foundation and a popular base. It has become a stance, viewpoint, and methodology that the Chinese need, acknowledge, and apply to their reality. Ultimately, it becomes interconnected with the essence of fine traditional Chinese culture and merges with the shared values people embrace daily intuitively.

Based on China's realities and looking toward modernization, globalization, and the future, China is consolidating the guiding role of Marxism in the ideological domain. Through the development of advanced socialist culture and the observation of socialist culture and ethical standards, China is promoting the creative transformation and innovative development of fine traditional Chinese culture. China integrates it into all aspects of social life, continuously helping the Chinese raise their political awareness and moral standards. This process also makes adapting Marxism to the Chinese context and the needs of our times more cohesive.

C. Integration Power: Making Efforts to Foster the "New Culture of the Chinese Nation" in the New Era

In January 1940, Mao Zedong raised the historical question of constructing the "new culture of the Chinese nation" in his article *On New Democracy*. At present, the proposal of the "Second Integration" has significantly expanded the direction, connotation, and space for adapting Marxism to the Chinese context and the needs of our times. Through the "Second Integration," a new path has been found to adapt Marxism to the Chinese context and the needs of the times, gradually merging it into the "new culture of the Chinese nation" in the new era.

Under the impetus of the "Second Integration", Marxism permeates into the discourse system of fine traditional Chinese culture, and the vitality of fine traditional Chinese culture is activated through the integration of the spirit of the times. Breaking free from the antithesis between "Marxism, China, and the West," Marxism, which has taken root in China for a century, now further embeds itself in the cultural soil of China through the "Second Integration".

Theoretical awareness and cultural confidence are the strength of a nation's progress; advanced values and a free mind are the source of social vitality. China has achieved a new leap forward in adapting Marxism to the Chinese context along the new trail blazed by the "Second Integration" by drawing from the concept and thinking of governing the country from fine traditional Chinese culture, and using Marxism as a guide in inheriting and developing such a culture in the contemporary era.

5. Creating New Forms: Contributing a New Chapter to Human Civilization

China's great social transformation is not a master-plate from which we simply continue our history and culture, nor a pattern from which we mechanically apply the ideas of classic Marxist authors, nor a reprint of the practice of socialism in other countries, nor a duplicate of modernization from abroad. The "Second Integration" deeply roots Marxism into fine traditional Chinese culture, making it an essential component of Chinese culture. It breaks free from the traditional confines of "Marxism with a Marxist soul, a Chinese body, and Western application." Instead, the integration has made each other successful, forming an organic and unified new cultural entity. It allowed Marxism to become Chinese, fine traditional Chinese culture to become modern, and the new culture developed through "integration" to become a cultural form of Chinese modernization.

A. From Integration to Reconstruction

Some theorists argue that the "Second Integration" theory is a significant original contribution like "putting new wine in a new bottle." The theory is not simply a mixture of Marxism and traditional Chinese culture, especially Confucianism, but rather a "chemical reaction" of activation and re-creation. It is a significant original contribution from a Chinese standpoint, breaking away from the Western discourse system.

Chinese modernization is the domain where the "Second Integration" is realized. Since the Opium War in 1840, modernization has become the goal pursued by numerous Chinese with lofty ideals. "How to achieve modernization and what kind of modernization to achieve" has been a question of the times. The "Second Integration" has calibrated the course and provided a clear direction for Chinese modernization.

The "Second Integration" takes a philosophical perspective on culture from the heights of human development and views it through the historical depth of China's 5,000-year civilization. The modernization of a country can only flourish and endure if it is rooted in the fertile soil of its own history and culture. The "Second Integration" integrates the Communist faith, socialist beliefs, and the millennia-old ideals of the Chinese nation, giving Chinese modernization a value orientation, cultural confidence, and historical support.

B. From Culture to Civilization

The "Second Integration" is not only a phenomenon of cultural integration but also a matter of civilizational fusion. The imprint of culture is embedded in all human activities of material production, invention, creation, and theoretical construction, giving rise to human civilization. Chinese modernization is deeply rooted in fine traditional Chinese culture, embodying the advanced essence of scientific socialism. It draws on the achievements of all human civilizations, represents the direction of progress in human civilization, and presents a new vision distinct from the Western model of modernization. It is an entirely new form of human civilization.

Chinese modernization builds upon the foundation of inheriting all the outstanding achievements of human civilization, from agricultural to industrial civilization. It incorporates the humanistic spirit embedded in the traditional Chinese culture, which advocates the idea of taking benevolence as a responsibility and "Do not do unto others what you would not want to be done unto you." It embraces the concept of unity between nature and humanity and respect for nature. It also incorporates the shared values of peace, development, fairness, justice, democracy, and freedom that belong to all human beings. In doing so, it achieves a significant breakthrough in transforming human civilization from industrial to modern.

According to the *Book of Documents*, a Chinese classic, "Great virtues carried forward can result in a harmonious clan, which will lead to a harmonious society, which, in turn, will lead to the harmony of all states." Thus, fine traditional Chinese culture has the distinctive characteristics of cosmopolitanism. Marxism has also advocated "global vision" and "humanistic care" since its birth. In his grasp of the general trend of the world, Xi Jinping keenly and profoundly captured this point of convergence and put forward the concept of "a human community with a shared future" from a far-sighted perspective. This concept is a Chinese idea and solution put forward with an eye on human development and the world's future. It conforms to the laws of the world's historical development and resonates with the universal aspirations of all humanity. Naturally, it has received wide acclaim and enthusiastic response from the international community.

C. From Adapting for Application to Excellence

Persistently integrating the basic tenets of Marxism with China's specific realities and fine traditional Chinese culture is a long-term historical process. The continuous integration of Marxism with Chinese civilization is opening up a great era of revitalizing Chinese civilization and human civilization at large. The "Second Integration" embodies the scientific decision and governance wisdom of Chinese leaders who accurately grasp both the interactions of conflicting global ideologies and cultures and profound changes in social and ideological concepts in Chinese society.

The revival of Chinese civilization can only be realized under the premise of the CPC's long-term governance in contemporary China. Without it, the so-called "cultural China" would have long ago withered away and become a "civilization in museums." The Chinese path has distinct characteristics determined by the historical heritage of thousands of years of Chinese civilization. However, the Chinese path is also universal, encompassing the general principles of scientific socialism established by Marx. Therefore, Xi Jinping emphasizes, "We uphold and develop socialism with Chinese characteristics and promote the coordinated development of material, political, ethical, social, and ecological civilizations. We have created a new path to modernization with Chinese characteristics and a new form of human civilization."

Marxism is the crystallization of advanced Western culture, originating from Western civilization yet transcending it with a broad cosmopolitan perspective. Since the introduction of Marxism into China, it has not only sparked profound changes in Chinese civilization but has also been gradually adapted to the Chinese context. Socialism with Chinese characteristics has revitalized the ancient Chinese civilization, infusing it with new vitality and vigor. It has significantly deepened the connotation and expanded the scope of Chinese civilization, propelling it to new heights.

Just as there are no bounds to practice, there is no end to theoretical innovation. It is the solemn historical responsibility of today's Chinese Communists to continue opening new chapters in adapting Marxism to the Chinese context and the needs of the times.

—Xi Jinping

Chapter III

Reliable Path to and Promotion Strategy for the "Second Integration"

Currently, the world is undergoing an unprecedented and accelerating transformation, and the historical process of the great rejuvenation of the Chinese nation is irreversible. The new development environment and historic mission require the CPC to scientifically apply the basic principles of Marxism, inherit and promote fine traditional Chinese culture, and promote the "Second Integration" to respond to new situations, address new challenges, meet new demands, promote new development, and embark on a new journey.

The "Second Integration" has opened up a new realm of adapting Marxism to the Chinese context and the needs of the times, representing today's essence of Chinese culture and the spirit of China. How to find the scientific path of the "Second Integration"? This report outlines ten aspects in this regard.

1. Upholding the Guiding Role of Marxism

As soon as it was established, the CPC firmly aligned itself with Marxism. Xi Jinping pointed out, "Marxism is the fundamental guiding ideology upon which our Party and country are founded; it is the very soul of our Party and the banner under which it strives." The Fourth Plenary Session of the 19th Central Committee of the CPC clearly stated the need to "highlight the fundamental system which ensures that Marxism guides all our ideological work" and decisively institutionalize the foundational system for ensuring the guiding role of Marxism in the ideological domain, elevating it to a fundamental national system and prioritizing it as a critical aspect of constructing an advanced socialist cultural system.

Only by having an accurate perspective of the foundational system for ensuring the guiding role of Marxism in the ideological domain can we effectively ensure the advancement of the "Second Integration" in the right direction. Upholding the fundamental system for ensuring the guiding role of Marxism, which is unique, essential, and institutional in the ideological domain, should never be shaken, obscured, or confused at any time. Throughout history, the downfall of many political parties, the collapse of many regimes, and the decline of many nations began with the confusion of guiding ideologies and the loss of leadership in the realm of ideology. This guiding position determines the nature and direction of socialist culture with Chinese characteristics. The creative transformation and innovative development of fine traditional Chinese culture must adhere to the guidance of Marxism; otherwise, we risk losing our direction.

2. Essential Attributes of Culture

Culture is the soul of a country and a nation. One fundamental attribute of culture lies in its values recognized by people. The competition of cultures is essentially one of values. China possesses firm confidence in its path, theories, and institutions, fundamentally rooted in the cultural confidence inherited over five thousand years of its civilization. Throughout its long evolutionary process, Chinese civilization has developed a unique system of values, cultural connotations, and spiritual qualities through which the Chinese people perceive the world, society, and the meaning of life. It is the fundamental characteristic that distinguishes China from other countries and nations, and it has forged the cultural confidence of the Chinese nation, which has been assimilating the strengths of various cultures.

Only by having an accurate perspective of the essential attributes of culture can we have a deeper understanding of the significance of the "Second Integration" in the great rejuvenation of the Chinese nation. Without a strong sense of cultural confidence and the flourishing of culture, there can be no realization of socialist modernization in China, nor can there be a great rejuvenation of the Chinese nation. Firm confidence in the path, theory, and system of socialism with Chinese characteristics ultimately stems from solid cultural confidence, which is also an important reason why the 1.4 billion Chinese people have formed strong cohesion. This has provided solid ideological guarantees and powerful inspiration for opening up new horizons for the cause of the Party and the country in the new era. The "Second Integration" is the CPC's profound summary of the historical experience of adapting Marxism to the Chinese context and the needs of our times. It reflects a deep understanding of the development laws of Chinese civilization, indicating that the CPC's knowledge of the Chinese path, theories, and institutions has reached new heights. It also signifies that the CPC's historical and cultural confidence has reached new heights and that its consciousness of promoting cultural innovation while inheriting fine traditional Chinese culture has reached new heights.

3. Fundamental Role of Culture

Culture is a spiritual force that can react to the material world and ultimately transform into a powerful material force. The soft power of culture can also be transformed into the hard power of the economy. A nation thrives when its culture thrives, and a nation becomes strong when its culture is strong. The capability of culture is deeply ingrained in a nation's vitality, creativity, and cohesion. The 5,000-year accumulation of Chinese civilization has brought tremendous confidence and pride to the Chinese people, serving as a source of unwavering spiritual strength.

Only by having an accurate perspective of the fundamental role of culture can we effectively unleash the tremendous strength generated by the "Second Integration" in the new journey of fully building a modern socialist China. In the new journey of fully building a modern socialist China, culture is an essential component of advancing the well-planned and coordinated efforts to implement the "Five-sphere Integrated Plan" (the five integrated areas are economic, political, cultural, social, and ecological) and the "Four-pronged Strategy" (the four prongs covering building a modern socialist country, expanding in-depth reform, promoting law-based governance, and enforcing strict Party self-governance). For that matter, culture is a significant fulcrum in promoting high-quality development, a crucial factor in meeting the growing aspirations of the people for a better life, and a significant source of strength in overcoming various risks and challenges on the path of progress. Integrating the basic tenets of Marxism with fine traditional Chinese culture will further unleash the fundamental role of culture and garner a magnificent force of unity in the nation's undertakings.

4. Positioning of Fine Traditional Chinese Culture

Fine traditional Chinese culture, created and continued by the Chinese nation in thousands of years of history, is the root and soul of the Chinese nation, an essential source for cultivating core socialist values, and a solid foundation for the Chinese nation to gain a firm footing in the global cultural interaction.

We can only enhance our historical consciousness and cultural confidence in the "Second Integration" by accurately understanding the positioning of fine traditional Chinese culture. "History and reality have shown that a nation that abandons or betrays its own history and culture not only fails to develop but also risks experiencing various historical tragedies." The 5,000-plus-year Chinese civilization carries the nation's spiritual heritage. Socialism with Chinese characteristics, with its distinctive features, takes root in the fertile soil of Chinese culture. Forgetting history, abandoning culture, and discarding traditions are equivalent to severing the spiritual lifeline of the Chinese nation. By firmly establishing cultural confidence and strengthening identification with Chinese culture, we can carry forward the excellent traditions with the spirit of the times. It will enable us to better build the Chinese ethos, values, and strength, endowing the path of socialism with Chinese characteristics with a profound historical heritage and unwavering determination for progress.

5. Intrinsic Laws of Cultural Inheritance and Development

Cultural inheritance and development follow inherent laws. They must adapt to the requirements of the development of the times and the needs of the people, and only creative transformation and innovative development can help achieve lasting cultural inheritance and development. Creative transformation transforms those connotations and outdated forms of expression that still have valuable lessons to offer in accordance with the characteristics and requirements of the times, endowing them with new contemporary meanings and forms of expression to restore their vitality. Innovative development means supplementing, expanding, and refining the connotations of traditional culture in line with the new progress and advancements of the times, enhancing its influence and appeal.

Only by having an accurate perspective of the inherent laws of cultural inheritance and development can we find scientific approaches and methods to promote the "Second Integration." By adhering to creative transformation and innovative development, we can activate the essence of fine traditional Chinese culture, promote the integration of the core of Marxist ideology with the essential elements of fine traditional Chinese culture, and integrate them with the shared values people unconsciously embrace in their daily lives. It is the only way to give scientific socialism theory a more distinctive Chinese character and provide a solid historical and popular foundation for adapting Marxism to the Chinese context and the needs of our times.

6. Best of Fine Traditional Chinese Culture

With a history stretching back to antiquity, fine traditional Chinese culture is extensive and profound; it is the crystallization of the wisdom of Chinese civilization. Traditional culture espouses many important principles and concepts, including pursuing the common good for all; regarding the people as the foundation of the state; governing by virtue; discarding the outdated in favor of the new; selecting officials based on merit; promoting harmony between humanity and nature; ceaselessly pursuing self-improvement; embracing the world with virtue; acting in good faith and being friendly to others; and fostering neighborliness. These maxims, which have taken shape over centuries of work and life, reflect the Chinese people's way of viewing the universe, the world, society, and morality. They have formed the essential characteristics and the development pattern of Chinese civilization, which features benevolence, emphasizes people's lives, respects justice and integrity, advocates righteousness, upholds universal harmony, and seeks common ground while agreeing to differences.

Only by having an accurate perspective of the essence of fine traditional Chinese culture can we find the source of vitality for the essence of the "Second Integration." Fine traditional Chinese culture is not only the spiritual lifeline of the Chinese nation but also an important source for nurturing core socialist values. The ideological concepts, values, humanistic spirit, and moral norms therein are the core elements of Chinese people's thoughts and psyche and significant value in addressing the issues of human society. Only by accurately grasping the best of fine traditional Chinese culture and understanding its essence can we better adapt the tenets of Marxism to fine traditional Chinese culture and further identify the objects and connotations to be integrated. On the one hand, we need to explore the up-to-date values of fine traditional Chinese culture and the common values of humanity. On the other hand, we need to present Marxism with more Chinese characteristics, style, and charm to root it in the land of China firmly.

7. Scientific Worldview and Methodology

Xi Jinping Thought on Socialism with Chinese Characteristics for a New Era, combining theory and practice, provides in-depth answers from entirely new perspectives to a series of major historical issues concerning the development of the Party and the country and the governance of the Party. It not only explains what needs to be done and why but also how to approach and address these issues. It provides strategic planning, tasks assignment, and problem-solving guidance, vividly reflecting the unity of Marxist worldview and methodology. It continuously puts forward new ideas, perspectives, and approaches that guide practical problem-solving. The scientific approach to advancing theoretical innovation requires adherence to putting people first, upholding self-confidence and self-reliance, advocating the principles while fostering innovation, focusing on problem-solving, adopting a systemic perspective, and embracing a global vision. These principles significantly embody the thought, viewpoint, and methodology of Xi

Jinping Thought on Socialism with Chinese Characteristics for a New Era.

Only by having an accurate perspective of the worldview and methodology of Xi Jinping Thought on Socialism with Chinese Characteristics for a New Era and persistently upholding and applying the principles, viewpoints, and methods embodied in it can we better understand the theoretical character and distinct features of the "Second Integration." It is based on the 5,000-year civilization of the Chinese nation, reflecting the defining features of Marxism and demonstrating distinctive Chinese features and characteristics of the times. Only by a deep understanding of its essence can we better meet the requirements of the times, correctly understand the problem, and effectively guide the practice.

8. High Compatibility between Fine Traditional Chinese Culture and Values of Scientific Socialism

The scientific socialist values contained in the basic tenets of Marxism are highly compatible with the values formed by the Chinese people through the ages. The core socialist values not only contain the essence of Marxism but also embody the essence of fine traditional Chinese culture. The encounter of Marxism and fine traditional

Chinese culture has revitalized and empowered both, enabling the former to take root and bear fruit.

Only by having an accurate perspective of the high compatibility between fine traditional Chinese culture and the advocacy of scientific socialist values can we build a bridge and bond for understanding the "Second Integration". The "Second Integration" is an important method and scientific path by which the adaptation of Marxism to the Chinese context and the needs of our times can enter a new realm. Only by finding the inherent relationship between the basic tenets of Marxism and fine traditional Chinese culture can we make them attract, activate, and promote each other, achieving a comprehensive integration of all the theories and principles of Marxism with fine traditional Chinese culture in all aspects and dimensions so that they will ultimately merge into one, making original contributions to the enrichment and development of Marxism.

9. Wisdom of Governance in Fine Traditional Chinese Culture

Fine traditional Chinese culture is an essential ideological and cultural source for the governance of the CPC. Over thousands of years, the Chinese nation has developed rich ideas about the system and governance of the state. Within the realm of fine traditional Chinese culture, there is a wealth of philosophical and social scientific content and wisdom in governance and statecraft. It provided an important foundation for ancient people to understand and transform the world and offers valuable references for us to uphold and improve socialism with Chinese characteristics and advance modernizing China's system and capacity for governance.

Only by having an accurate perspective of the governance wisdom contained in fine traditional Chinese culture can we clarify the historical positioning of the "Second Integration" in modernizing China's system and capacity for governance. In governing China, the CPC respects history and culture, rejecting historical and cultural nihilism. It neither forgets the heritage of history nor belittles Chinese culture. The CPC is adept at drawing wisdom from fine traditional culture to govern the country and benefit the people. At the same time, it observes, grasps, and leads the times from the standpoints, viewpoints, and methods of Marxism, constantly deepening the understanding of the laws underlying governance by a communist party, the building of socialism, and the development of human society. These are crucial experiences of the Party in its endeavor to govern the country and rejuvenate the nation. They are also practical explorations to achieve the "Second Integration."

10. Trends of Exchanges and Mutual Learning between Civilizations

Exchange and mutual learning are essential requirements for the development of civilizations. The diverse paths to modernization taken by different countries and regions today are rooted in rich and enduring cultural heritages. The various civilizations created by human societies shine brilliantly, endowing each country's modernization with profound heritage and distinctive characteristics. These civilizations transcend time and national boundaries, making significant contributions to the progress of human society collectively.

Only by having an accurate perspective of the trend of exchange and mutual learning among world civilizations can we promote the "Second Integration" and make more outstanding global contributions in building a human community with a shared future and promoting common values for all humanity. All things coexist and flourish without harming one another, and various paths run parallel without conflicting with each other. In promoting the development and progress of human civilization, China not only contributes to the emergence of new forms of civilization but also offers new concepts of civilization. Peace, development, fairness, justice, democracy, and freedom, these common values of humanity, are the core concepts of fine traditional Chinese culture that transcend time and space, shining upon every corner of the world. China is also committed to promoting the exchange and mutual learning of civilizations, aiming to overcome estrangement between civilizations with exchanges, prevent their clash with mutual learning, and overcome a false sense of superiority with coexistence. China encourages countries worldwide to value the inheritance and innovation of their own historical cultures, explore the contemporary values of their cultural heritages, and promote the continuous progress of human civilization.

The peaceful nature of Chinese civilization fundamentally determines that China will continue to build world peace, contribute to global development and safeguard the international order, and that it will continue to pursue exchanges and mutual learning among civilizations rather than cultural hegemony. It also determines that China will not impose its own values and political system on others. China is a champion of cooperation, not confrontation. Never will it dish out favors to acolytes and punishments to opponents.

—Xi Jinping

Chapter IV

Global Significance and Inspiration for the Times from the "Second Integration"

To the international audience, the "Second Integration" embodies China's way of governance by the power of culture. It answers the "What makes China" question from the governance perspective. By adhering to the "Second Integration," the power of Marxism has revitalized the Chinese civilization. At the same time, Marxism itself gains nourishment from the fertile soil of fine traditional Chinese culture. It has acquired distinct Chinese characteristics, styles, and grandeur. It shows the world that the Chinese path to modernization and the new forms of human civilization it has created are deeply rooted in its historical culture and civilization traditions. Based on this historical and cultural heritage, modern China stands firm as a responsible major power, providing stability and certainty amid changes in the world, the era, and history. It represents a progressive force committed to upholding world peace and development.

Based on the new era and looking toward the future, the Chinese path of governance provides insights into the peaceful coexistence of civilizations in the 21st century and offers inspiration for countries to build a better world jointly.

1. China's Commitment to World Peace and Stability with Cultural Strength

The "Second Integration" theory's proposal is an intellectual endeavor of China in the context of unprecedented changes in the world and China's commitment to great rejuvenation of the Chinese nation. Under the guidance of this theory, China has transitioned from cultural self-awareness to cultural self-confidence and further to cultural self-strengthening. It reflects the vision of Chinese leaders since the 18th National Congress of the CPC, as they have stood at the forefront of the times, looked ahead, and worked towards the grand vision of building a human community with a shared future. They have led the Chinese people to upgrade their understanding, transform their thinking, and update their concepts, providing a logically consistent interpretation of governance in China. With the power of culture and civilization, China plays a constructive role in safeguarding world peace and stability.

A. Reconstructing Historical Perspectives: Going Beyond Old Ideas and Taking the Initiative to Innovate

For a long time, the narratives about China in world history have been dominated by such perspectives as "stagnation theory," "cyclical theory," and "backwardness theory." While China's modernization has been progressing rapidly, the understanding of Chinese history and culture, both domestically and internationally, has not kept pace with the development of the times.

Scholar Zheng Yongnian believes that for a culture to become a "soft power," it must be able to explain itself and enable "others" to understand and be convinced, ultimately leading to "others" voluntary acceptance.[1]

The "Second Integration" theory goes beyond the Western-centric perspective that has prevailed in modern times and the old notions within China itself. It reconstructs the Chinese people's understanding of their own history and effectively explains the current

---

[1] Zheng Yongnian, *The Revival of Chinese Civilization*, The Eastern Publishing Co., Ltd., 2018, p188.

success of China. As a result, it enables the Chinese people to seize the historical initiative and have the mindset of taking the initiative. This transformative perspective has already influenced people with a breadth of vision in other developing countries.

"Even understanding China, we see it from the prism of the West, but then things began to change." On March 25, 2023, during the Asia Youth Leaders Forum's opening ceremony of in Guangzhou, Malaysia's Prime Minister Anwar bin Ibrahim stated in a video speech: "Look at how we understand our cultures. We always feel the West is superior. We were always told that to progress, we must be one of them. But we realize that this cannot be the case. We started looking at our own experience, our own history, and our own contributions of our forefathers."

B. Reshaping Identity: Addressing the Challenges of Our Time, Resolving Identity Confusion

The current world faces an identity crisis in politics, with the emergence of tribalism within nations and a fault line in the world order of globalization, as stated by American political scientist Francis Fukuyama in recent years.[1]

---

[1] Francis Fukuyama (US), *Identity: The Demand for Dignity and the Politics of Resentment*, China Translation & Publishing House, 2021.

Many scholars argue that Western-style modernization has led people to an atomized life, causing them to have a sense of loss. People in all countries are looking for a "sense of belonging," and countries are looking for "recognition." The struggle toward "recognition" focuses on identity. It has led to greater challenges in a country's internal governance and more complex exchanges between countries.

Through the "Second Integration" theory, Chinese leaders have reshaped their country's cultural identity and social consensus, thereby strengthening national and political identity. With cultural self-confidence under the leadership of the CPC, the Chinese have further reinforced confidence in their path, theory, and system.

C. Reinterpreting Civilization: Constructing the Chinese Narrative and Promoting Civilizational Exchange

Today, the "clash of civilizations" notion is still widely popular worldwide. Western centrism and white supremacy may have changed their appearance over time, but their core has not changed in essence. The two-way confrontation between the "civilized" world dominated by the West and "non-civilized" forces affects the trend of international relations.

From elaborating on China's concept of civilization to an international audience on occasions such as delivering a speech at the UNESCO headquarters to proposing the Conference on Dialogue of Asian Civilizations, Xi Jinping has repeatedly expounded on the significance of cultural exchange and mutual learning to the world. Civilizations may vary in manifestations but should never be judged in superiority or inferiority. Faced with notions like the clash of civilizations and racial supremacy, China firmly advocates respecting each other's history, national conditions, and development paths. It emphasizes the need for cultural exchange to transcend cultural barriers, mutual learning to transcend conflicts, and coexistence to go beyond claims of superiority.

At the CPC in Dialogue with World Political Parties High-level Meeting held in March 2023, Xi Jinping put forward the Global Civilization Initiative, emphasizing the promotion of cultural exchange and mutual learning. This initiative further enriches and expands the practical path toward building a human community with a shared future.

2. Chinese Way of Governance: Managing Challenges from the Six Dialectical Relationships

The report to the 20th National Congress of the CPC put forward the "Six Upholds": upholding the people-centered approach, upholding self-confidence and self-reliance, upholding fundamental principles while breaking new ground, upholding a problem-oriented approach, applying systems thinking, and maintaining a broad vision. These reflect Xi Jinping's worldview and methodology of socialism with Chinese characteristics in the new era and serve as a vivid embodiment of the theory of the "Second Integration." This "six-in-one" methodology reveals the six dialectical relationships between theory and practice in China's governance in the new era. It represents the modern development of China's traditional thinking and reflects Marxist dialectical materialism. It provides a valuable reference for other countries striving to address governance challenges.

A. The Relationship Between the People and the Entity

Ancient Greek philosopher Aristotle once said that man is, by nature, a political animal. Only through shared living can individuals become fully realized as humans in the truest sense. From an ontological perspective, humans exist in relation to one another, and none can exist outside of these relationships.

In modern society, the key to good governance for managing public life lies in handling the relationships with the "people". No ruling party in the world does not mention the "people". in its reports and speeches, but it is uncommon for them to prioritize the people's interests above all else and put them first in governance practice.

Chinese leaders' emphasis on "putting the people at the center" differs from the "people-based" concept under the context of "bureaucracy centered on officials" in ancient China or the Western emphasis on individual rights. It is also distinct from the God-centered religious concept or the capital-centered idea prevalent in capitalist societies. From the perspective of governance in China, the people occupy the top position and become a legitimate source of ontological significance.

In March 2019, during his state visit to Italy, Xi Jinping said: " I will put aside my own well-being for the good of my people." On February 20, 2021, Xi Jinping stated at the mobilization meeting to study Party history: "This country is its people; the people are the country." The report to the 20th National Congress of the CPC emphasized the need to stand firmly with the people, respond to their wishes, respect their creativity, and pool their wisdom.

Surveys conducted by overseas institutions such as Harvard University's Belfer Center consistently show that the CPC has enjoyed an approval rate of over 90 percent among the Chinese people for many years. Compared to political parties worldwide, such a level of governance achievement is rarely seen.

B. The Relationship between Self-reliance and Learning from the Overseas

China's stability, unity, and prosperity today may be impossible without learning from other countries and being open to the world. However, the fundamental reason for China's achievements lies in the fact that the Chinese people refuse to be subordinate to other countries and persist in independently carving out their own path.

"China's issues must be dealt with by Chinese people in light of the Chinese context," as stated in the report to the 20th National Congress of the CPC. The CPC forged the path to success in China today as it leads the people through independent exploration, and the Chinese chapter of Marxism was written by the Chinese Communists relying on their own strength in practice. China must adapt to changes without being closed and rigid. Simultaneously, the country cannot simply copy and imitate foreign ideas without digesting them.

"Where there is a transition from nonexistence to existence, opening up new prospects and pioneering new paths, there is inevitably a manifestation of spiritual presence at its origin," said historian Qian Mu.[1]

The "Second Integration" theory finds the cultural source of this self-confidence, self-reliance, and self-improvement.

---

[1] Qian Mu, *Chinese Cultural Spirit*, Jiuzhou Press, 2012, p97.

C. The Relationship between Innovation and Upholding Fundamental Principles

"Although Zhou was an old state, its mission lies in reform," as the classical *Book of Songs* chanted. The spirit of "constant innovation" formed in China since ancient times has extended theoretically in the "Second Integration" of the new era.

Innovation should be based on upholding fundamental principles. By adhering to the tenets of Marxism, grasping the principles of socialism with Chinese characteristics, and embracing the new trend of the times, China will not lose its direction or deviate from its course.

How can the "Second Integration" theory be transformed into a driving force for practical development? Xi Jinping has proposed creative transformation and innovative development of fine traditional Chinese culture. This approach is not only applied in the narrow sense of the cultural industry and undertakings. Still, it is gradually embedded in the governance practices of various fields in China, including politics, economy, society, and culture.

D. The Relationship between Problems and Theories

Problems are the precursors of theories, while theories are a distillation of problems. It is necessary to discover problems in practice, summarize theories, and use them to guide practice in transforming reality.

How to pinpoint and identify problems? Where to find them? The report to the 20th CPC National Congress focuses on five key areas: new problems encountered in practice; deep-rooted problems intrinsic in reform, development, and stability; pressing issues concerning the people's immediate interests; significant issues in the international context; and prominent issues facing the Party's growth. Exploring these problem areas reflects Chinese leaders' close integration of theory and practical issues and their profound insights into the national and global circumstances. It is a fundamental approach to the success of China's governance by the power of culture.

E. The Relationship between the System of the Whole and the Part

Traditional Chinese thinking has a holistic and interconnected nature. Chinese people believe that everything is interconnected and interdependent. We can only grasp an object or event's laws of development by viewing them with the understanding that they are universally connected, part of a complete system, and constantly evolving.

This holistic, comprehensive, and systematic way of thinking can transcend partial, sub-disciplined, and specific thinking, allowing the

Chinese to rise above temporary and particular issues, enabling them to understand the relationships between the present and the future, the whole and the part, and the small and the large.

Xi Jinping has repeatedly emphasized the importance of bearing in mind the country's most fundamental interests and cultivating a "systematic way of thinking."

"Chinese people have a strong aptitude for a global perspective, much like appreciating a landscape painting, where they first focus on the overall picture before examining the details." This observation was made by Joshua Cooper Ramo, vice chairman and CEO of Kissinger Associates, an international geopolitical consulting firm based in the United States.

F. The Relationship between China and the World

"We must cultivate moral character and prioritize education to attract people outside China." That has been the tradition guiding China's interactions with the world. "Having a global perspective" is what the CPC members cherish.

Unlike the Western worldview that sees the world as something to be conquered, the Chinese people have traditionally understood the world as "*tianxia*" (all under Heaven), an ancient concept of the world. Whether "governing the world per the requirements of world governance"[1] or "observing the world from the world's perspective"[2] means using the world as the yardstick to understand the world as a political organic whole. It is the principle of "there being no distinction between nations." In the eyes of the Chinese people, any external existence is seen as an issue to be addressed rather than an object to be conquered.[3]

Under the vision of building a human community with a shared future, the CPC not only seeks happiness for the Chinese people and rejuvenation for the Chinese nation but also strives for progress for humanity and the world. It aims to broaden its global perspective, deeply understand the trends of human development and improvement, actively respond to the shared concerns of people from all countries, and contribute to addressing the common challenges facing humanity. With an inclusive and open-minded approach, it draws upon and absorbs the achievements of all civilizations to promote the construction of a better world.

A better world contributes to a better China, and a better China leads to a better world. In the new era, China engages itself with the

---

[1] *Guanzi: Herdsmen*
[2] Laozi: The Fifth-fourth Chapter of *Tao Te Ching*.
[3] Zhao Tingyang, "Contemporaneity of the World: Practice and Imagination of World Order," CITIC Publishing Group, 2016 edition, page 5.

world with a mindset of interconnection, interdependence, win-win cooperation, and harmonious co-existence.

3. Harmonious Coexistence: Contributing to a Better Future with a New Form of Human Advancement

At the celebration of the 100th anniversary of the founding of the CPC, Xi Jinping pointed out, "As we have upheld and developed socialism with Chinese characteristics and driven coordinated progress in material, political, cultural-ethical, social, and ecological terms, we have pioneered a new and uniquely Chinese path to modernization, and created a new form of human advancement." The new form of human civilization is the crystallization of the CPC's adherence to the "Two Integrations" in its unremitting struggle to lead the Chinese people to achieve national rejuvenation and promote modernization through a Chinese path. From the metaphysical "*dao*" (principles) to the physical "*qi*" (concrete things), this new form of civilization has already reached different levels and generated tremendous positive effects worldwide.

A. The Way of Concept: New insights into the Ideal Society of the World

American scholar Philip Clayton believes that the world is

facing a series of crises that capitalism can never resolve. Three significant consensuses have emerged globally: the ecological crisis, the consequences of unregulated capitalism, and the "death of modernity."[1]

Clayton, who has conducted in-depth research on Chinese issues, believes that Xi Jinping Thought on Socialism with Chinese Characteristics for a New Era holds great significance in addressing the common challenges of human society.

In an era of globalization with escalating predictable and unpredictable risks and challenges, what constitutes the ideal state of the international community? How should we envision the common future of humanity?

History has shown that how leaders envision the world often determines its reality. Under the concept of a human community with a shared future, China envisions a magnificent world characterized by "lasting peace, universal security, common prosperity, openness and inclusiveness, and a clean and beautiful environment."

From 2013 to 2023, Chinese leaders have put forward a series of new concepts and ideas that focus on the global perspective and are

---

[1] Philip Clayton and Justin Heinzekehr, *Organic Marxism: An Alternative to Capitalism and Ecological Catastrophe (Toward Ecological Civilization)*, translated by Meng Xianli, Yu Guifeng, and Zhang Lixia, People's Press, 2015, p14.

oriented towards the world: the concept of a human community with a shared future, the new type of international relations, the shared values of all humanity, the Global Development Initiative, the Global Security Initiative, and the Global Civilization Initiative.

From confusion, negligence, and even smear and attack, to serious attention, thorough research, and broad participation, the responses from countries worldwide to what China put forward have greatly changed over the past decade.

On September 18, 2018, during his meeting with a visiting head of state, Xi Jinping said, "China advocates building a human community with a shared future, which means advocating mutual respect, equality, diversity, and win-win cooperation among countries. As the Chinese saying goes, everything has its strengths and weaknesses. Regardless of their size, all countries have their own merits and are equal members of the international community. We should reject the law of the jungle where the strong prey on the weak and the winner takes all."

"Harmony in diversity" and "Everything has its strengths and weakness" are both ideas rooted in fine traditional Chinese culture and embody the essence of Marxist dialectical materialism. Different civilizations should mutually respect each other, seek common ground while reserving differences, coexist harmoniously, transcend supremacy through the co-existence of civilizations, and go beyond conflicts through mutual understanding and exchange.

Xi Jinping said, "To build a human community with a shared future is not to replace one system or civilization with another. Instead, it is about countries with different social systems, ideologies, histories, cultures, and levels of development coming together for shared interests, shared rights, and shared responsibilities in global affairs, and creating the greatest synergy for building a better world."[1]

Carlos Martinez, a British writer and China researcher, stated that China's economic strength and global status have significantly increased in the past decade. China's foreign policy aligns with the international community's demand for peace, progress, and sustainable development and the requirements for building a human community with a shared future. It starkly contrasts with the Cold War policies centered around consolidating hegemony.

B. The Instrument of Practice: The Implementation Mechanism of Integrating Knowledge and Action

Integrating Marxism with fine traditional Chinese culture needs

---

[1] Xinhua News Agency, "Xi Jinping Attends the Commemoration Ceremony of the 50th Anniversary of the Restoration of the People's Republic of China's Lawful Seat in the United Nations and Delivers an Important Speech," October 25, 2021.

Chapter IV Global Significance and Inspiration for the Times from the "Second Integration"

to be put into practice.

Over the past decade, Chinese leaders have continuously put forward new ideas and concepts in diplomacy while implementing these ideas in practice. Xi Jinping, as head of the state, made scores of foreign visits and China held many milestone diplomatic events. These include the G20 Summit, the BRICS Summit, the China International Import Expo, the China-ASEAN Expo, the United Nations Biodiversity Conference, the Global Conference on Cyberspace, and many others. China has enhanced its cultural confidence by hosting or playing a major role in various international events, and its contributions to civilization have reached far and wide.

The China-proposed Belt and Road Initiative, developed for a decade, represents the "materialization" of China's new form of human civilization in the global development arena. It is a significant public good China contributes to the world's peaceful development.

In August 2018, on the 5th anniversary of advancing the Belt and Road Initiative, Xi Jinping used traditional Chinese painting skills to explain how to improve the Belt and Road Initiative from "*daxieyi*" (freehand brushwork) to "*gongbihua*" (meticulous brushwork). In April 2019, at the second Belt and Road Forum for International Cooperation, Xi Jinping put forward the goal of advancing the Belt and Road Initiative in the direction of high-quality development.

According to the latest statistics from the "Belt and Road" Portal of China, by January 6, 2023, China had signed over 200 cooperation documents for jointly building the Belt and Road Initiative with 151 countries and 32 international organizations. Initiatives such as the China-Europe Railway Express, the Asian Infrastructure Investment Bank (AIIB), the Silk Road Fund, and various bilateral and multilateral cooperation mechanisms under the Chinese proposal are flourishing. Over the past decade, this initiative has transformed from an idea to actions, from vision to reality.

Italian scholar Giovanni Andornino said the Belt and Road Initiative had shaped China's identity as a global leader and reorganized the existing world order in a non-hegemonic manner.[1] Former Japanese Prime Minister Shinzo Abe had said that the Belt and Road Initiative had profound historical significance in maintaining world peace and stability, promoting cultural diversity, and fostering sustainable development of human civilization.[2]

The new form of human civilization created by China is guided

---

[1] Giovanni B. Andornino, "The Belt and Road Initiative in China's Emerging Grand Strategy of Connective Leadership," *China & World Economy*, Vol.25, No.5, 2017.

[2] "Promoting the New Development of China-Japan Relations," *People's Daily*, October 27, 2018.

by the value pursuit of fulfilling the people's aspirations for a better life. It embodies the cultural genes featuring the beliefs that "all the people are my brothers and I share the life of all creatures" and "all nations should live in harmony." It is significant and offers inspiration for the modernization efforts of developing countries.

In the complex and turbulent world undergoing drastic changes unseen in a century, even established developed countries are facing new development needs. According to Gustaaf Geeraerts, director of the Contemporary China Research Institute in Brussels, Belgium, China is not only a developing country but also a major emerging power, and these two roles will eventually fuse China into a "responsible great power." In fact, visionary politicians have already taken proactive actions.

On April 7, 2023, Xi Jinping and his French counterpart Emmanuel Macron, who was visiting Guangzhou, enjoyed a performance of the renowned ancient Chinese piece "High Mountains and Flowing Water", played on a Tang Dynasty Guqin by a Chinese musician. Xi told Macron that a touching story about friendship lies behind this ancient Chinese Guqin melody, passed down for thousands of years.

Under the guidance of the theory of the "Second Integration", Marxism of contemporary China is showing vigorous vitality. Chinese modernization keeps unfolding with grandeur. This new form of human civilization created by China greets the world with a friendly attitude.

"China will open its arms wider to embrace the world and contribute more dynamic achievements of its civilization to a better world in the future."[1]

---

[1] "Keynote Speech by Xi Jinping at the Opening Ceremony of the Conference on Dialogue of Asian Civilizations," Xinhua News Agency, May 15, 2019.

Conclusion

The "Second Integration" answers the questions of "where does it come from" and "where it is going" concerning the governance of China. It is a theory and a series of practices that point not only to the present but also to the future. Only with the "Second Integration" can we explain China's historical legitimacy, governance capacity, and vitality. Without a deep understanding of the Chinese civilization that has been developing for over 5,000 years, it is impossible to fully recognize China as a major force for safeguarding world peace and development.

In the era of accelerating changes unseen in a century on a global scale, to fully build a modern socialist China and advance national rejuvenation, China needs to keep advancing the "Second Integration" based on the significant achievements and valuable experience already attained in this regard.

The adaptation of Marxism to the Chinese context and the needs of the times will continue.

Writing Explanation and Acknowledgements

The think tank report "Toward modernization: The value of Xi Jinping's Economic Thought" is led by Fu Hua, President of Xinhua News Agency and Chairman of the Academic Committee of Xinhua News Agency's New China Research (NCR), as the head of the project team; Lyu Yansong, the Chief Editor, as the team's deputy head; and Zhao Cheng, former Vice President of Xinhua News Agency, as the executive deputy head. Other members of the project team include Liu Gang, Zhang Xudong, Cui Feng, Li Xingwen, Zou Wei, Fu Yunwei, Ye Qian, Xu Yang, Han Jie, An Bei, Yu Jiaxin, Yang Liu, Fu Yan, He Zongyu, Yuan Junbao, He Xinrong, Zhang Ziyun, Liu Hongxia, Chen Gang, Kong Xiangxin, Liang Jianqiang, Tu Hongchang, Deng Qian, Chen Yongrong, Zhou Yuan, Liu Mingxia, Gao Lu, and others.

Since its initiation in June 2022, the project has taken more than 8 months for study, research, writing, revision, and proofreading. During the process of report writing and release, various departments and institutions such as the Office of the Central Commission for Financial and Economic Affairs, Chinese Academy of Social Sciences (CASS), Policy Research Office of the National Development Commission, Xi Jinping Economic Thought Research Center, and others, as well as experts and scholars including Gao Peiyong, Vice President of Chinese Academy of Social Sciences (CASS) and Secretary of the Party Committee of CASS University, Ma Yuan, Vice Secretary General of CASS, Zhang Yong, Director-General of the Secretariat of the Office of the Central Commission for Financial and Economic Affairs, Li Yu, Deputy Director of the Economic Bureau of the Central Policy Research Office, Meng Wei, Deputy Director of the Policy Research Office of the National Development Commission, Spokesperson, Shi Yulong, Director of the Xi Jinping Economic Thought Research Center, Feng Weijiang, Deputy Director of the Institute of World Economics and Politics at CASS, Guo Liyan, Director of the Comprehensive Situation Research Office at the China Macroeconomic Research Institute, Liu Ruiming, Assistant Dean of the National Development and Strategic Research Institute at Renmin University of China, have provided valuable assistance and guidance.

We extend our heartfelt gratitude to all of them. While writing this report, due to the limitations of available materials and the expertise of the authors, errors and omissions are inevitable. We sincerely welcome criticism and corrections from our readers.

▸ 改变中国的"第二个结合" ▸ 建设中华民族现代文明的理论创新与实践

Project Team and Acknowledgments

"The Second Integration" That Transforms China—Theoretical Innovation and Practice in Building the Modern Civilization of the Chinese Nation think-tank report is led by Fu Hua, President of Xinhua News Agency and Chairman of the Academic Committee of Xinhua News Agency's New China Research (NCR), as the head of the project team; Lü Yansong, the Chief Editor, as the team's deputy head; and Zhao Cheng, former Vice President of Xinhua News Agency, as the executive deputy head. Other members of the project team include Liu Gang, Chu Guoqiang, Xiao Chunfei, Cui Feng, Liu Lina, Fu Yan, Li Jinfeng, Liang Jianqiang, Lin Hui, Liu Xiangxiao, Yang Yimiao, Wang Bo, Wurihan, Feng Yuan, Yan Rui, Tong Fang, Zhang Yunlong, Xu

Zhuang, Guo Honghai, Xu Xueyi, Feng Zixiong, Ma Changbao, Liu Aihong, He Huiyuan, and Liang Jin.

The project has taken five months to complete since its inception in February 2023, involving studying, researching, writing, revising, and reviewing.

While writing and releasing the report, we received all kinds of help and guidance from many experts and scholars. We want to express our sincere gratitude to them. They include Wang Junwei, Director of the Academic and Editorial Committee of the CPC Central Institute of Party History and Literature; Li Junru, former Vice President of the Party School of the CPC Central Committee; Zhang Zhiqiang, Director of the Philosophy Institute of the Chinese Academy of Social Sciences; Yu Yunquan, Dean of the Academy of Contemporary China and World Studies at the China International Communications Group; Zang Fengyu, Dean of the Philosophy Institute at Renmin University of China; Sun Xiguo, Executive Vice Dean of the Institute for Xi Jinping Thought on Socialism with Chinese Characteristics for a New Era at Peking University; Wang Xuebin, Director of the Chinese History Research Office of Department of History and Literature at the Party School of the CPC Central Committee; Xiong Chengyu, Director of the Institute of Cultural Development at the Communication University of China;

Weng Hekai, Deputy Director of the Department of Chinese Culture Teaching and Research at the Central Institute of Socialism; and Gao Changwu, Associate Editor of *CPC's Historical Documents* at the CPC Central Institute of Party History and Literature.